Readers' Theater, Grade 3: Science and Social Studies Topics

Contents

Introduction

Readers' Theater: Science and Social Studies is a program that provides engaging fluency instruction for all your readers!

Students at different reading levels

- Practice the same selections
- Pursue the same instructional goals
- Interact and build fluency together!

Students build fluency through readers' theater plays on science or social studies topics.

Each play has four to six character roles at different reading levels (measured by the Flesch-Kincaid readability scale). Use the reading levels as a guide, not a rule. In some instances, the readability levels may be somewhat misleading, as they are determined in part by syllable count. If a multi-syllable word is repeated frequently in a character's role, the role appears to be at a high reading level. Once the student masters the word, that part of the role is no longer as challenging.

The instructional power of the small mixed-ability group is at the heart of this program. Each play and lesson plan has been carefully designed to promote meaningful group interaction. In contrast to independent reading, readers using *Readers' Theater* build skills in a rich environment of peer-to-peer modeling, discussion, and feedback.

The program provides a clear, structured approach to building fluency, vocabulary, and comprehension. The key to developing skills is practice. Each lesson provides that practice through a routine of five instructionally focused rehearsals.

1. The first rehearsal focuses on familiarizing the students with the overall text.

2. The Vocabulary Rehearsal involves students in various activities focusing on vocabulary words. Use the Word Cards blackline on page 9 to help students master the vocabulary.

3. The Fluency Rehearsal provides explicit fluency instruction focused on one of the following skill areas:
   - Phrasing Properly
   - Reading with Word Accuracy
   - Using Expression
   - Using Punctuation

4. The Comprehension Rehearsal provides explicit comprehension instruction focused on one of the following skill areas:
   - Asking Questions
   - Building Background
   - Identifying Main Idea
   - Making Connections
   - Making Inferences
   - Monitoring Comprehension
   - Summarizing
   - Visualizing

5. The Final Rehearsal brings it all together.

Following the Final Rehearsal, students will be able to perform the play with great confidence and success. Use the Individual Fluency Record on page 8 to provide students with positive feedback.

Features

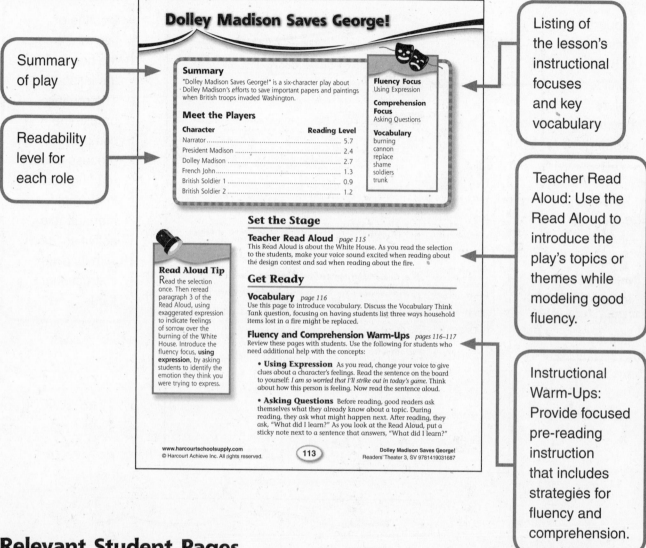

Summary of play

Readability level for each role

Dolley Madison Saves George!

Summary

"Dolley Madison Saves George!" is a six-character play about Dolley Madison's efforts to save important papers and paintings when British troops invaded Washington.

Meet the Players

Character	Reading Level
Narrator	5.7
President Madison	2.4
Dolley Madison	2.7
French John	1.3
British Soldier 1	0.9
British Soldier 2	1.2

Fluency Focus
Using Expression

Comprehension Focus
Asking Questions

Vocabulary
burning
cannon
replace
shame
soldiers
trunk

Set the Stage

Teacher Read Aloud *page 115*
This Read Aloud is about the White House. As you read the selection to the students, make your voice sound excited when reading about the design contest and sad when reading about the fire.

Get Ready

Vocabulary *page 116*
Use this page to introduce vocabulary. Discuss the Vocabulary Think Tank question, focusing on having students list three ways household items lost in a fire might be replaced.

Fluency and Comprehension Warm-Ups *pages 116–117*
Review these pages with students. Use the following for students who need additional help with the concepts:

• **Using Expression** As you read, change your voice to give clues about a character's feelings. Read the sentence on the board to yourself: *I am so worried that I'll strike out in today's game.* Think about how this person is feeling. Now read the sentence aloud.

• **Asking Questions** Before reading, good readers ask themselves what they already know about a topic. During reading, they ask what might happen next. After reading, they ask, "What did I learn?" As you look at the Read Aloud, put a sticky note next to a sentence that answers, "What did I learn?"

Read Aloud Tip
Read the selection once. Then reread paragraph 3 of the Read Aloud, using exaggerated expression to indicate feelings of sorrow over the burning of the White House. Introduce the fluency focus, **using expression**, by asking students to identify the emotion they think you were trying to express.

113

Dolley Madison Saves George!
Readers' Theater 3, SV 9781419031687

Listing of the lesson's instructional focuses and key vocabulary

Teacher Read Aloud: Use the Read Aloud to introduce the play's topics or themes while modeling good fluency.

Instructional Warm-Ups: Provide focused pre-reading instruction that includes strategies for fluency and comprehension.

Relevant Student Pages

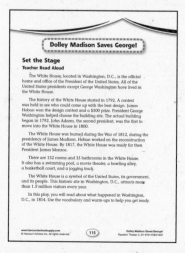

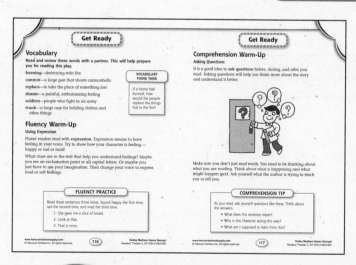

Features, *continued*

Opportunity for students to build confidence before beginning group work

Tip for engaging student groups in another meaningful vocabulary activity

Vocabulary Tip
For more vocabulary practice, have students discuss the following:
- Which would make you feel **shame**: lying to a friend or helping a family member?
- Would an elephant fit into a **trunk**? Would a book?
- What do you own that would be hard to **replace**?

Routine of five rehearsals, the heart of the lesson. The routine breaks the complex process of oral reading down into simple, manageable activities, each with its own instructional focus.

Dolley Madison Saves George! *pages 118–124*

Independent Practice
Set up the groups and assign each student a part. Then have students read through their assigned parts once before small group practice begins.

Small Group Practice
Assemble the groups. You may want to use the following rehearsal schedule. Each rehearsal, which should involve a complete oral read-through, has an activity to guide students.

1. First Rehearsal: Guide students to preview the play by reading the title, character list, and stage directions. Invite a volunteer to use the title to predict George's identity. Invite students to then read together as a group for the first time.

2. Vocabulary Rehearsal: Direct students to locate and list on index cards the vocabulary words used in the play. Have them turn the cards facedown and take turns choosing a card and pantomiming the word for other members of the group to guess.

3. Fluency Rehearsal: Using Expression Before the rehearsal begins, invite students to review the Fluency Tips by alternating reading them aloud. Then encourage students to have fun by overacting—exaggerating characters' feelings. Explain that the narrator can overact by using a deep voice and reading the lines as if giving an important news broadcast.

4. Comprehension Rehearsal: Asking Questions After this rehearsal, have students work together to answer this question: What are we supposed to learn from this play? Ask them to list at least three facts they think the author wanted to teach through the play.

5. Final Rehearsal: Observe this rehearsal, focusing on students' expression. For example, when reading French John's line on page 120, "I could put a cannon at the gate!" does the student read with excitement?

Performance
This is your opportunity to sit back, relax, and enjoy the performance. Encourage students to have fun while performing!

Curtain Call *pages 125–126*
Assign these questions and activities for students to complete in a group or independently.

114

Dolley Madison Saves George!
Readers' Theater 3, SV 9781419031687

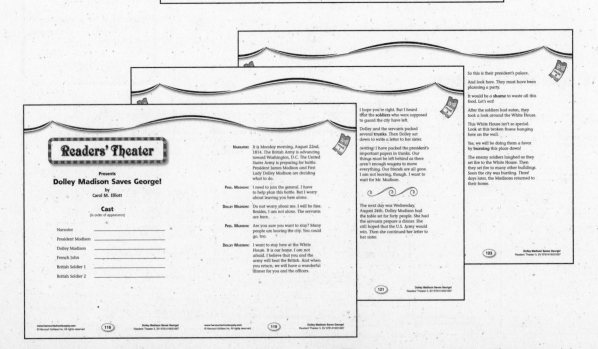

Readers' Theater 3, SV 9781419031687

Features, *continued*

Comprehension questions ranging from literal to inferential

Name _____ Date _____

Comprehension

Write your answer to each question on the lines below.

1. Why was President Madison worried about leaving his wife?

_____

_____

2. How did French John help Dolley Madison?

_____

_____

3. What did the British soldiers do when they saw the table set for dinner?

_____

_____

4. Why did Dolley Madison tell French John to break the frame on Washington's picture? _____

5. Why did Dolley Madison feel she needed to save the painting of George Washington? _____

6. What would you ask the author if you could talk to her?

_____

_____

7. Why do you think the British wanted to burn the White House?

_____

(125)
Dolley Madison Saves George!
Readers' Theater 3, SV 9781419031687

Name _____ Date _____

Vocabulary

Write the vocabulary word that answers the question.

trunk	soldiers	cannon	shame	burning	replace

1. Which word describes people who fight for their country? _____

2. Which word names a weapon? _____

3. Which word can be a suitcase or part of a tree? _____

4. Which word is the opposite of *pride*? _____

5. Which word can describe a fire? _____

Extension

1. What would you have done if you were Dolley Madison and the British were coming? With a partner, talk about what you would have done.
   - How long would you have stayed in the White House?
   - What would you have tried to save?
   Write a short play telling your ideas.

2. With a partner, do some research on Washington, D.C., and write a story about it. Then read your story aloud to the class. Choose a topic below.
   - Write a story about one of the famous people or buildings in the city.
   - Write a story about what it would be like, or is like, to live in D.C.
   Use the web on page 13 to help you.

3. Research the major wars in United States history. Place them on the time line on page 14.

(126)
Dolley Madison Saves George!
Readers' Theater 3, SV 9781419031687

Vocabulary items testing students' understanding, not their ability to identify verbatim definitions

Extension activities for additional interaction, involvement, research, writing, and creativity. Use the blackline masters provided on pages 9–14 to help students complete these extension activities.

Index of Reading Comprehension and Fluency Skills

Reading Comprehension Skills

Skill	Play	Pages
Asking Questions	The Fourth Rock from the Sun	57–70
	Dolley Madison Saves George!	113–126
Building Background	The Worst Thanksgiving Ever	71–84
	Don't Be Afraid	99–112
Identifying Main Idea	Plant and Gator Soup	29–42
	A Day at the Weather Center	43–56
Summarizing	The No-Sleep Sleepover	15–28
	The Tallest Tale Ever	85–98

Fluency Skills

Skill	Play	Pages
Phrasing Properly	The No-Sleep Sleepover	15–28
	The Tallest Tale Ever	85–98
Reading with Word Accuracy	The Worst Thanksgiving Ever	71–84
	Don't Be Afraid	99–112
Using Expression	The Fourth Rock from the Sun	57–70
	Dolley Madison Saves George!	113–126
Using Punctuation	Plant and Gator Soup	29–42
	A Day at the Weather Center	43–56

Readers' Theater 3, SV 9781419031687

Correlation to Standards

Unit 1: Science

The No-Sleep Sleepover *Pages 15–28*

Science Standards: Knows the common characteristics of groups of vertebrate animals
   Understands the various ways that animals depend on plants for survival

Plant and Gator Soup *Pages 29–42*

Science Standards: Understands the various ways that animals depend on plants for survival
   Knows behavioral and structural adaptations that allow plants and animals to survive

A Day at the Weather Center *Pages 43–56*

Science Standards: Understands characteristics of weather
   Recognizes patterns in weather
   Knows that scientists and technologists use a variety of tools to obtain information

The Fourth Rock from the Sun *Pages 57–70*

Science Standard: Knows characteristics of Earth and Mars

Unit 2: Social Studies

The Worst Thanksgiving Ever *Pages 71–84*

Social Studies Standard: Explains the significance of selected ethnic and cultural celebrations

The Tallest Tale Ever *Pages 85–98*

Social Studies Standard: Understands the importance of writers and artists to the cultural heritage of communities

Don't Be Afraid *Pages 99–112*

Social Studies Standard: Uses problem-solving and decision-making skills, working independently and with others, in a variety of settings

Dolley Madison Saves George! *Pages 113–126*

Social Studies Standards: Is familiar with important American heroes from the past
   Knows the history of important national landmarks

Name _____   **Date** _____

Individual Fluency Record

	Needs Improvement	Satisfactory	Excellent
Expression			
Uses correct intonation for statements			
Uses correct intonation for questions			
Uses correct intonation for commands			
Uses correct intonation for exclamations			
Interjects character's emotions and moods			
Reads words in all capitals to express character's emotions			
Reads words in dark print to express character's emotions			
Reads onomatopoeia words to mimic character			
Volume			
Uses appropriate loudness			
Voice reflects tone of character			
Voice reflects feelings of character			
Accuracy			
Reads words accurately			
Speed			
Reads sentences smoothly with line breaks			
Reads words in short sentences as meaningful units			
Reads phrases and clauses as meaningful units			
Reads rhyming text at a constant speed			
Reads rhythmic text with a constant beat			
Punctuation			
Pauses at the end of sentences			
Pauses at commas that follow introductory phrases			
Pauses at commas in series			
Pauses at commas in clauses			
Pauses at commas after introductory names			
Pauses at ellipses			
Pauses at dashes			
Recognizes that question marks are questions			
Recognizes that exclamation points indicate strong feeling			
General			
Demonstrates confidence			
Feels at ease in front of an audience			
Speaks without being prompted			
Speaks at the appropriate time for the character's part			
Demonstrates the character's personality			
Teacher Comments			

Blackline Master: Individual Fluency Record
Readers' Theater 3, SV 9781419031687

WHAT IS THE WORD?

Write the word here.

_____

WHAT DOES THE WORD MEAN?

Write the meaning here.

_____

_____

_____

_____

_____

WHAT DOES THE WORD STAND FOR?

Draw a picture of it here.

HOW CAN YOU USE THE WORD?

Write a sentence using the word here.

_____

_____

_____

_____

_____

Blackline Master: Word Cards
Readers' Theater 3, SV 9781419031687

Characteristics (What They Have or Do)		

Things to Compare

Weather Watch

Keep track of the temperature in your town for 1 week. At the same time each day, guess what you believe the outside temperature is. Check a thermometer to see what the temperature actually is. Then listen to the radio to hear what your local meteorologist says the temperature is.

Using 3 different colors, plot a 3-line graph showing your estimates, your thermometer readings, and the meteorologist's report for the week. Include a color key and a title. Are your lines close?

Title: _____   **Key:** _____

Fahrenheit Degrees	Monday	Tuesday	Wednesday	Thursday	Friday
100					
95					
90					
85					
80					
75					
70					
65					
60					
55					
50					
45					
40					
35					
30					
25					
20					
15					
10					
5					
0					

Days

Blackline Master: Line Graph
Readers' Theater 3, SV 9781419031687

Name _____   Date _____

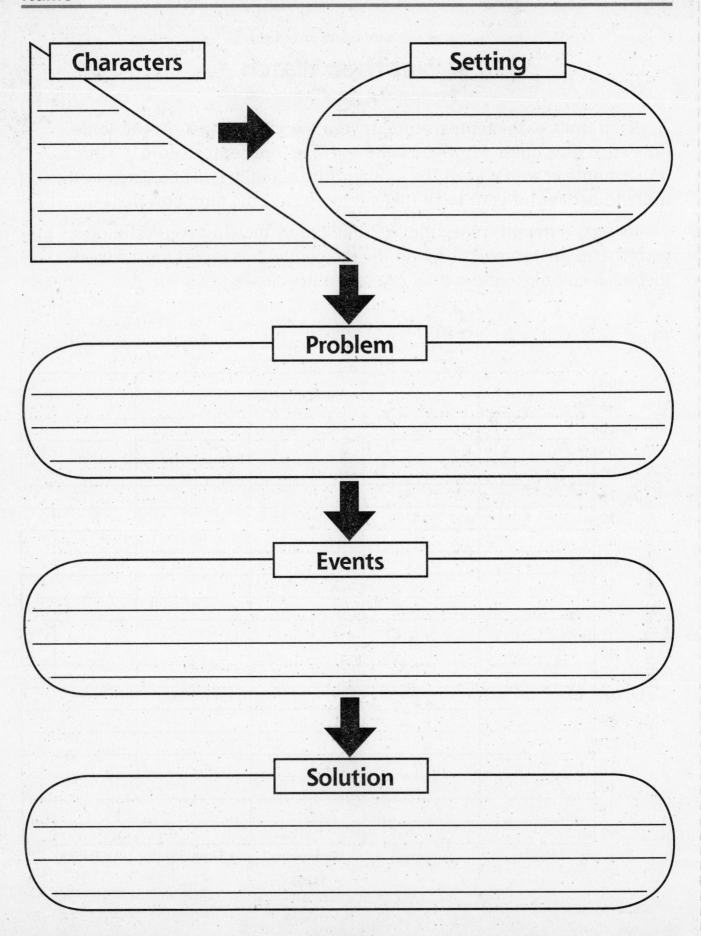

Characters

Setting

Problem

Events

Solution

Blackline Master: Story Map
Readers' Theater 3, SV 9781419031687

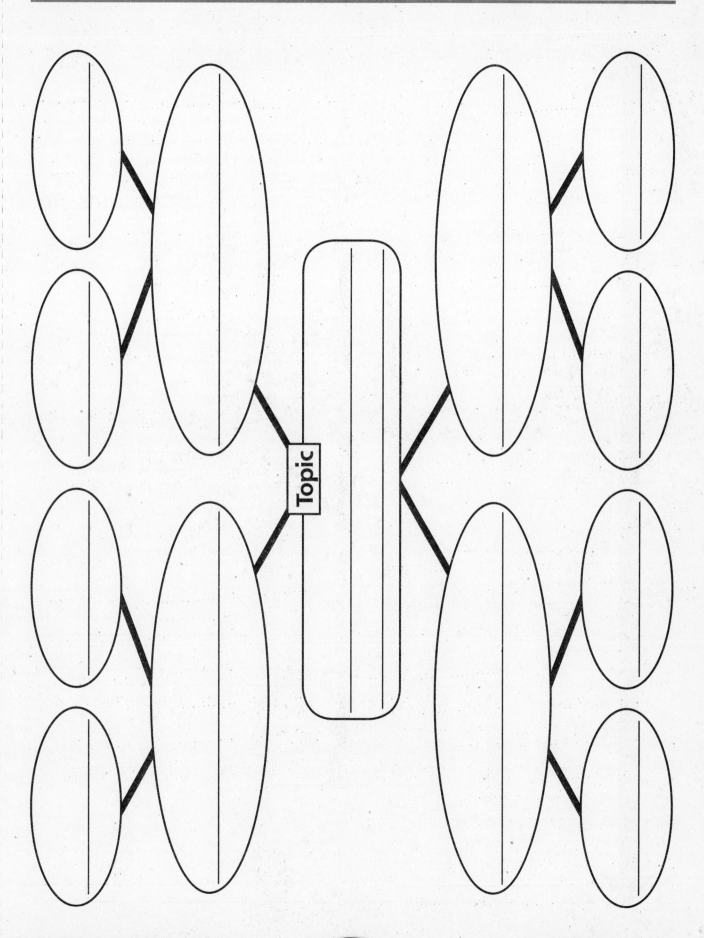

13

Blackline Master: Idea Web
Readers' Theater 3, SV 9781419031687

Name _____

The No-Sleep Sleepover

Summary

"The No-Sleep Sleepover" is a five-character play about a young bear that invites two friends for a sleepover and then discovers that his pals don't sleep at night!

Meet the Players

Character	Reading Level
Bruno Bear	1.2
Father Bear	2.2
Raymond Raccoon	1.1
Sergio Squirrel	1.4
Orville Owl	0.1

Fluency Focus
Phrasing Properly

Comprehension Focus
Summarizing

Vocabulary
adventure
bury/burying
favorite
gather/gathering
guest
twitch/twitching

Read Aloud Tip

Explain that the fluency focus of **phrasing properly** involves reading in phrases, or chunks, rather than one word at a time. Point out that in the first sentence in the Read Aloud, the phrases are separated by commas. Read the sentence twice, first stressing the phrase boundaries by pausing longer than normal, and then modeling how to read the phrases smoothly in sequence.

Set the Stage

Teacher Read Aloud   *page 17*

This selection is about nocturnal animals. Ask students to listen carefully to the phrasing as you read the selection aloud.

Get Ready

Vocabulary   *page 18*

Use this page to introduce vocabulary. Discuss the Vocabulary Think Tank question. Challenge students to support their choices by giving two reasons why a particular animal is their favorite.

Fluency and Comprehension Warm-Ups   *pages 18–19*

Review these pages with students. Use the following for students who need additional help with the concepts:

- **Phrasing Properly** Look at the first sentence in paragraph 4 of the Read Aloud. Now listen to two ways of phrasing the sentence: *What animals might—you find working at—night?* Now listen to this: *What animals—might you find—working at night?* Which phrasing is easier to understand?

- **Summarizing** Summarizing is retelling the important parts of what you read. Look at paragraph 3 of the Read Aloud. Name two or three of the most important ideas in the paragraph. Put those ideas together in a one-sentence summary of the paragraph.

The No-Sleep Sleepover *pages 20–26*

Independent Practice

Set up the groups and assign each student a part. Then have students read through their assigned parts once before small group practice begins.

Small Group Practice

Assemble the groups. You may want to use the following rehearsal schedule. Each rehearsal, which should involve a complete oral read-through, has an activity to guide students.

1. First Rehearsal: Have students note the words in italics. Explain that these words are stage directions that tell readers how to speak or what to do, or that explain an event. For example, when the stage directions say *They hear a scratch at the door,* the student playing Raymond Raccoon should make a scratching noise.

2. Vocabulary Rehearsal: Have students locate the vocabulary words used in the play and write each on a separate index card. Then invite students to take turns choosing and displaying a card, reading the word aloud to the group, and using it in a sentence.

3. Fluency Rehearsal: Phrasing Properly Have students review page 18. Then for the rehearsal, designate one student to be the tip reader. At the end of pages 22, 25, and 26, ask the tip reader to read the tip aloud. After the reading, have volunteers choose one tip and model using it as a guide for reading a line of the play.

4. Comprehension Rehearsal: Summarizing Have students work together to list three important ideas from the play. Challenge the groups to use these ideas to write a three-sentence summary.

5. Final Rehearsal: Observe this rehearsal, focusing on students' phrasing. For example, when Father Bear reads his first lines, does the student pause at each punctuation mark?

Performance

This is your opportunity to sit back, relax, and enjoy the performance. Encourage students to have fun while performing!

Curtain Call *pages 27–28*

Assign these questions and activities for students to complete independently or in a group.

Vocabulary Tip

For more vocabulary practice, have students discuss the following:

- What could you **gather** in the woods? On the beach?

- Which is more of an **adventure**—going to the grocery store or going on a hike in the mountains? Why?

- Would you like to have more or less of your **favorite** food? Why?

The No-Sleep Sleepover

Set the Stage
Teacher Read Aloud

Each night, after most people are in bed, many animals are just waking up. These creatures of the night are beginning their work—hunting for food, finding mates, or caring for their young. In the morning, an overturned garbage can or fresh tracks in the snow tell us that something has been busy in the night.

Why do these creatures prefer the darkness? Many animals are nocturnal because they are protected against heat and dryness at night, they can hide more easily from their enemies, and they have less competition for food.

How do these animals survive in the dark? Many have extra-sharp vision. Their large eyes collect all possible light. Others have powerful hearing or a sense of smell that directs them. Some have sensors that locate a prey by its body heat. Others use echolocation, which is a method of finding things with sound. Echolocation guides animals even in total darkness.

What animals might you find working at night? You may see a cat prowling down the alley, with its special eyes for seeing in the dark. That little rabbit out in the garden has special hearing. Those bats that you see around lampposts can use echolocation to help them find their way.

In this play, you will read about some interesting animals. Use the vocabulary and warm-ups to help you get ready.

Get Ready

Vocabulary

Read and review these vocabulary words to prepare you for reading this play. Say each word aloud two times.

adventure—an unusual or exciting experience

bury/burying—to hide under the ground and cover

favorite—preferred above all others

gather/gathering—to pick up from many sources

guest—a visitor

twitch/twitching—to move with a quick motion

> **VOCABULARY THINK TANK**
>
> Tell a friend about your favorite animal.

Fluency Warm-Up

Phrasing Properly

To be a fluent reader, try to read in chunks, or **phrases**. Reading one word at a time sounds dull. It also makes the meaning of the sentence hard to understand. Meaning comes from phrases, not individual words.

There are many times when punctuation will help you phrase properly. However, sometimes you will have to figure out phrasing on your own. The more you practice reading aloud, the more you will learn to make natural breaks in the text.

> **FLUENCY PRACTICE**
>
> Read this sentence one word at a time, without proper phrasing. Then group words together and read the sentence again.
>
> I—went—to—the—eye—doctor—today—for—an—eye—exam.

Comprehension Warm-Up

Summarizing

To **summarize** means to retell the important parts of the story. When you retell a story, you tell about the characters and what happened.

Take breaks throughout the reading to check your understanding of the story. Keep notes for your summary.

COMPREHENSION TIP

As you read, ask yourself questions like these below.

1. What does the title tell me?
2. What is the main problem or conflict?
3. How is the problem solved?

Readers' Theater

Presents

The No-Sleep Sleepover

by
Justine Dunn

Cast

(in order of appearance)

Bruno Bear _____

Father Bear _____

Raymond Raccoon _____

Sergio Squirrel _____

Orville Owl _____

Bruno Bear: *(shouting)* Dad! Dad! Hurry! My friends will be here any minute! I'm so excited! I'm having a sleepover!

Father Bear: I know you're excited, Bruno, but I have to finish making the snacks. You have very hungry friends!

Bruno Bear: I know, Dad. I just want to make sure we have time to go on an **adventure**. This is going to be the best sleepover ever!

Father Bear: We will have plenty of time. Your friends will be here all night.

(They hear a scratch at the door.)

Raymond Raccoon: Hi, Bruno. Can I come in?

Bruno Bear: Hi, Raymond! Sure, come on in. You can leave your mask at the door. *(Laughs.)*

Raymond Raccoon: Very funny, Bruno. You know I can't take my mask off. It's part of my fur.

Bruno Bear: I'm just kidding. Let's go to my den. I want to show you my new computer game!

The No-Sleep Sleepover
Readers' Theater 3, SV 9781419031687

RAYMOND RACCOON: Cool! I can't wait to play it!

FATHER BEAR: Good to see you, Raymond. Be sure to listen for your other **guests** at the door. (*He walks into the other room.*)

RAYMOND RACCOON: Who else is coming, Bruno?

BRUNO BEAR: Sergio Squirrel and Orville Owl will be here soon. (*They hear another scratch at the door.*)

SERGIO SQUIRREL: Hi, guys. Can I come in?

BRUNO BEAR: Hi, Sergio. We were just talking about you. Was your tail **twitching**? (*Laughs.*)

✳ **SERGIO SQUIRREL:** No, I only twitch my tail when I'm worried.

RAYMOND RACCOON: Sergio, you're just in time. We are going to play a computer game.

SERGIO SQUIRREL: That sounds like fun! Bruno, can I leave my seeds here in the kitchen? I don't want to carry them around in my cheeks all night.

BRUNO BEAR: Sure, Sergio. You can put your seeds with the snacks my dad made us.

> ✳ **FLUENCY TIP**
>
> Practice phrasing one of Sergio Squirrel's lines like this: *No—I only— twitch my tail— when I'm worried.*

FATHER BEAR: *(coming back into the room)* Hello, Sergio. I'm so glad you could come over. How are your parents?

SERGIO SQUIRREL: My parents are great, thanks. My dad has been **gathering** nuts and seeds for winter. My mom has been busy **burying** them.

RAYMOND RACCOON: Do you eat anything besides nuts and seeds, Sergio?

SERGIO SQUIRREL: Sometimes I eat berries or insects, but nuts and seeds are my **favorite**. What do you eat?

RAYMOND RACCOON: I really like fish, frogs, and crabs. How about you, Bruno?

BRUNO BEAR: My favorites are ants and honey. But I also eat seeds, nuts, berries, and fish just like you guys.

ORVILLE OWL: *(flies in through an open window)* Whoooooo is talking about food?

FATHER BEAR: Orville Owl! We didn't even hear you coming because you fly so quietly.

SERGIO SQUIRREL: We were just talking about food. What are your favorites, Orville?

ORVILLE OWL: I like to eat small birds and mice.

FATHER BEAR: I hope you still enjoy the snacks I made.

ORVILLE OWL: I'm not hungry. I just ate.

FATHER BEAR: You don't have to eat the snacks now. Why don't you go on your adventure?

ORVILLE OWL: Where are we going?

SERGIO SQUIRREL: Let's go into the forest and play hide and seek!

RAYMOND RACCOON: What about the computer game?

ORVILLE OWL: I'm not very good at those.

BRUNO BEAR: We can play a game another time. It's getting late, so let's go on our adventure.

(The group of friends goes outside.)

SERGIO SQUIRREL: I'm a little tired. I'm usually in bed by now.

ORVILLE OWL: I stay up at night.

RAYMOND RACCOON: I like to be awake at night, too. Where should we go?

The No-Sleep Sleepover
Readers' Theater 3, SV 9781419031687

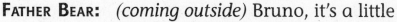

FATHER BEAR: *(coming outside)* Bruno, it's a little late for you and your friends to be out alone. Come inside for a snack. I made everyone's favorites.

BRUNO BEAR: *(whining)* But Dad, we didn't get to go on our adventure.

ORVILLE OWL: That's OK, Bruno. I'm hungry now.

SERGIO SQUIRREL: I'm hungry, too. Let's go eat.

(The group comes back inside and sees the snacks.)

ORVILLE OWL: Thank you, Mr. Bear.

BRUNO BEAR, RAYMOND RACCOON, AND SERGIO SQUIRREL:
(in unison) Yes, thank you!

FATHER BEAR: You're welcome. When you're finished with your snacks, it will be time to go to sleep.

ORVILLE OWL: Mr. Bear, I stay awake at night. I sleep during the day.

RAYMOND RACCOON: I stay awake at night, too. Usually I look for food with my parents.

BRUNO BEAR: Dad, can't we stay up late, just this one time?

FLUENCY TIP

For proper phrasing, make sure you take a breath whenever you see end punctuation.

FATHER BEAR: I guess that would be OK. If you stay awake all night, this won't really be a sleepover.

SERGIO SQUIRREL: I want to try to stay awake, too.

ORVILLE OWL: Let's watch a movie.

RAYMOND RACCOON: Let's play a game.

SERGIO SQUIRREL: Let's build a fort.

BRUNO BEAR: This is the best no-sleep sleepover ever!

(The group laughs.)

FLUENCY TIP

If something doesn't make sense, try rereading the sentence.

Comprehension

Write your answer to each question on the lines below.

1. How are Bruno Bear and his father different from Raymond Raccoon and Orville Owl?

_____

_____

2. What do Raymond Raccoon and Orville Owl usually do at night?

_____

_____

3. Father Bear says he made everyone a favorite snack. Name a food he might have made for each of the friends.

_____

_____

4. Tell two facts you learned about animals.

_____

_____

5. Who was your favorite character in this play?

_____

_____

6. How would you summarize what happened in the play?

_____

_____

Vocabulary

Write the vocabulary word that answers each question.

> bury   guest   twitching   gather   adventure   favorite

1. Which word describes an exciting experience? _____

2. Which word means the opposite of *dig up*? _____

3. What do you call someone who is invited to your house? _____

4. Which word tells an action a tail can make? _____

5. Which word describes something you like best of all? _____

Extension

1. In a small group, research habits of other animals. Then use a chart to present your findings to the class.

SAMPLE "ANIMAL HABITS" CHART		
ANIMAL	WHAT IT EATS	WHERE IT SLEEPS
bear	fish	den

Or, you can use the chart on page 10.

2. With a partner, talk about your idea of a perfect party.

   • What favorite foods would you eat?

   • If you could invite a famous person as a guest, who would you invite?

   • What else would you do at the perfect party?

Plant and Gator Soup

Summary

"Plant and Gator Soup" is a five-character play about a family whose visit to the Everglades results in one family member experiencing a much-too-close encounter with a gator.

Meet the Players

Character	Reading Level
Narrator	3.9
Dad	2.1
Sarah	0.9
Max	0.5
Ranger	3.4

Fluency Focus
Using Punctuation

Comprehension Focus
Identifying Main Idea

Vocabulary
adapt
Everglades
carnivorous
clever
wetland

Set the Stage

Teacher Read Aloud *page 31*

This selection is about Everglades National Park. Read the selection aloud, modeling good fluency. At the end of each paragraph, stop and reread one sentence, asking students to read along with you.

Get Ready

Read Aloud Tip

After reading the selection once, introduce the fluency focus of **using punctuation**. Then point out that a dash indicates a pause. Direct students' attention to paragraph 2 of the Read Aloud. Ask for a volunteer to read aloud the sentence that includes a dash.

Vocabulary *page 32*

Use this page to introduce vocabulary. Discuss the Vocabulary Think Tank question. Ask students to support their answers with facts. For example, a student might say, "I am not *carnivorous* because I am a vegetarian. Vegetarians don't eat meat."

Fluency and Comprehension Warm-Ups *pages 32–33*

Review these pages with students. Use the following for students who need additional help with the concepts:

- **Using Punctuation** Paying attention to punctuation helps you know how to read a selection. Always remember to pause when you come to a comma. Study paragraph 3 of the Read Aloud to find commas. Read the last sentence of the paragraph together, pausing at each comma.

- **Identifying Main Idea** The main idea describes what a text is mostly about. Look at paragraph 2 of the Read Aloud. What is the most important information in this paragraph? Write one sentence that gives that information.

Plant and Gator Soup *pages 34–40*

Independent Practice
Set up the groups and assign each student a part. Then have students read through their assigned parts once before small group practice begins.

Small Group Practice
Assemble the groups. You may want to use the following rehearsal schedule. Each rehearsal, which should involve a complete oral read-through, has an activity to guide students.

1. First Rehearsal: Have students read the title and cast of characters and look at the illustrations in the play. Ask volunteers to predict where the play takes place and what happens to the characters. Then have students read together as a group for the first time.

2. Vocabulary Rehearsal: Before this rehearsal, ask each student to create a dictionary entry for one vocabulary word from the play. Each entry should include the word, an explanation of its meaning, an illustration, and a sentence using the word. Provide the blackline master on page 9. Give students time to share their dictionary entries with one another.

3. Fluency Rehearsal: Using Punctuation During this rehearsal, encourage students to pay attention to the Fluency Tips. Ask them also to note question marks and exclamation points in their lines and to read these lines in a questioning voice or an excited one, as appropriate. After the rehearsal, invite students to choose one question or exclamation to read aloud to the group.

4. Comprehension Rehearsal: Identifying Main Idea Ask groups to list at least ten of the most important details about the play. Then challenge groups to use the details to write one sentence that describes the main idea of the entire play.

5. Final Rehearsal: Observe this rehearsal, focusing on students' use of punctuation. For example, when Max says, "BUZZZ! OUCH!" does the student say the words in an excited voice? When needed, model using punctuation correctly for students having difficulty.

Performance
This is your opportunity to sit back, relax, and enjoy the performance. Encourage students to have fun while performing!

Curtain Call *pages 41–42*
Assign these questions and activities for students to complete in a group or independently.

Vocabulary Tip
For more vocabulary practice, have students discuss the following:

- List three **carnivorous** animals. Tell how you know each animal is carnivorous.

- What do you do to **adapt** yourself to very cold weather?

Plant and Gator Soup

Set the Stage
Teacher Read Aloud

The Everglades National Park is the only subtropical forest preserve in North America. The park is found at the southern part of Florida. The climate and wetland environment combine to create an area rich in plant and animal life. In fact, the Everglades is the only place in the world where you can see crocodiles and alligators living next to each other.

A man named Ernest F. Coe is known as the father of the Everglades. In 1928, he was the first to work toward creating a national park in southern Florida. He wanted to protect the glades that seemed to go on forever—the Everglades. He had heard of rare animals being hunted and rare beautiful flowers being picked there. President Franklin Roosevelt approved his request in May 1934.

It took years for the land to be properly acquired and for boundaries to be set. The park was officially dedicated in 1947 by President Harry Truman. In 1996, the new Everglades National Park Visitor Center was named the Ernest F. Coe Visitor Center, in honor of the person who worked toward the preservation of the Everglades.

You will read a play that takes place in the Everglades and learn about some interesting plants that live there and the ways they adapt to their environment. Use the vocabulary and warm-ups to help you get ready.

Vocabulary

Read and review these vocabulary words to prepare you for reading this play. Three of these words are in the Read Aloud on page 31. Which ones?

adapt—to change or adjust

Everglades—swampy national park in southern Florida

carnivorous (car NIV er us)—meat-eating

clever—skillful and smart

wetland—low-lying area partly covered with water; swamp or marsh

VOCABULARY THINK TANK

Are you carnivorous?

Fluency Warm-Up

Using Punctuation

Fluent readers pay attention to **punctuation**. They know where the punctuation is and what it stands for. You need to change the way you read based on the punctuation.

When you get to a punctuation mark, don't skip it and race forward. Stop at periods. Pause at commas. Use your question voice at a question mark. Express excitement at an exclamation point.

FLUENCY PRACTICE

Read these sentences aloud. Pause when you see a comma.

1. After school, buses need to be careful.
2. The week before, she lost a tooth.
3. I like to eat hotdogs, pudding, and fruit.

Comprehension Warm-Up

Identifying Main Idea

When you identify the **main idea** in a text, you find what is most important. Sometimes writers state the main idea directly. When writers don't state the main idea directly, you have to find clues in the text.

The title is sometimes a clue. Pictures are clues. Bold words are clues to important words. Reading is a little like being a detective!

COMPREHENSION TIP

As you read, add up the clues to get to the main idea.

    Clue 1: What is the title?

    Clue 2: What words are bold?

    Clue 3: What's in the pictures?

    Main Idea: What is important to remember?

Readers' Theater

Presents

Plant and Gator Soup

by
Laura Layton Strom

Cast

(in order of appearance)

Narrator _____

Dad _____

Sarah _____

Max _____

Ranger _____

NARRATOR: A family is sitting at the dinner table discussing their day.

DAD: Mom called tonight. She is going to have to stay in Boston an extra week. Her company needs her there a little longer.

SARAH: Oh, rats! We planned to go to the movies this weekend.

DAD: Well, all is not lost. I have an idea for something better than a movie for this weekend. Let's drive down to the **Everglades**!

SARAH: Cool! I have seen the Everglades on TV.

MAX: What is the Everglades?

DAD: The Everglades is a national park. It is in south Florida. It is a **wetland**, with miles of grassy water. It is 50 miles wide. It is only 1 to 3 feet deep. In fact most of the water is only 6 inches deep! You will see all kinds of interesting plants and animals.

MAX: Sounds boring.

DAD: Do you think alligators and snakes are boring? How about plants that eat meat?

MAX: No! Does the park have those?

DAD: Yes, it sure does.

MAX: Dad, I would LOVE to see an alligator. How soon can we leave! Can we camp?

DAD: That's the positive attitude I hoped for. A friend at work has an aunt who is a ranger there. She has a spare cabin we can stay in. She said she will guide us through the park. We can leave in the morning.

NARRATOR: The next evening, the family arrives at the rangers' cabins.

SARAH: I've never seen a darker night in my whole life.

MAX: It sure is noisy out here. Bugs are clicking and buzzing under every leaf. BUZZZ! OUCH! That's my first Everglades bug bite.

DAD: You have to wear bug spray in the Everglades.

NARRATOR: The family walks up a creaky boardwalk that leads to the cabins. The only lights are the moon and the ruby red eyes of alligators in a nearby swamp. Grasses and plants slap at the family's ankles as they walk. Soon they see warmly lit windows ahead.

> ❋ **FLUENCY TIP**
>
> Stress the words in all capital letters.

SARAH: Finally! I was getting worried.

MAX: *(tripping)* Ugh! Someone needs to trim the bushes around here.

NARRATOR: The family knocks on the door, and Ranger Meléndez answers.

RANGER: Well, hello, and welcome to the Everglades. Please come in. I've just prepared dinner, so please join me. I made gator nuggets, cornbread hush puppies, and lima beans.

MAX: Gator nuggets?

RANGER: Yes, they are a special food of Florida. They are quite tasty.

MAX: OK. I'll try it. I'll show that gator who's boss!

NARRATOR: The next morning, the group gets up early. The boat trip begins at five A.M. They put on hats, sunglasses, sunscreen, and bug spray. They put the boat into the water and get in.

DAD: Wow! I've never seen such a beautiful sunrise. There are so many different shades of pink and purple.

MAX: Look at this river, everybody. It looks like a maze. I bet you could get lost in here.

RANGER: Yes, I've been lost before. It is just one little waterway after another. The grasses are so high. You can't see around the corner.

SARAH: Dad said that there are **carnivorous** plants here. They eat meat. Can you show us some?

DAD: Yes, I read that there are bladderworts here.

RANGER: Yes, bladderworts float in the water. There are some right there. *(Pointing.)* See there are hundreds of tiny bladders on the stem. Bladders are clear hollow bags about the size of a pinhead. Each of those bags is a trap that catches small animals.

DAD: Look closely. You can see water fleas inside some of the traps.

SARAH: Ugh. That is so sick.

RANGER: No, that is how the **clever** bladderwort **adapts** to living in water.

MAX: *(dragging his hand along the weeds)* Ouch, that grass bit me!

FLUENCY TIP

Take a breath after each period. Otherwise you will run out of air in the wrong places.

Plant and Gator Soup
Readers' Theater 3, SV 9781419031687

RANGER: It's called sawgrass for a reason. It is sharp like the edge of a saw. Sawgrass is all over the Everglades. Here's a bandage.

SARAH: What other strange plants can you show us?

RANGER: *(pointing)* See that plant? The coontie looks like a small palm tree. The early native people made flour from the coontie plant. The coontie is sometimes called Florida arrowroot. I've had arrowroot cookies, and they are tasty.

MAX: Weird! I would not guess you could make cookies from that plant. *(Points to small island of alligators.)* Look at those lazy gators! They are so slow. They don't scare me.

DAD: Alligators can move very fast. They lift up on their toes. They can run 30 miles per hour. That's as fast as your school bus goes on Main Street!

✳ **SARAH:** My dad used to swim with alligators!

DAD: Yes, but that was when I was a kid. *(Looks at Ranger.)* I grew up in Florida. We swam in ponds near our house. We kicked and splashed a lot to keep the gators away.

RANGER: Alligators can be quite mean. And it is illegal to bother them in the Everglades.

MAX: I've got to get a picture of this. *(Jumps up.)*

NARRATOR: The boat begins to tip toward the island of alligators. Max topples out of the boat, SPLASH! He is eye to eye with a twelve-foot gator. Max tries to stand up in the thick, plant soup. Just then, Ranger Meléndez plucks him up and puts him back in the boat. The gator looks bored.

RANGER: Best to do as you are told next time, Max.

MAX: *(shaking with fear)* Yes, ma'am. Thank you.

NARRATOR: The group heads back to the cabin. Max cleans up while Ranger Meléndez and Dad make lunch. Everyone waits at the table as Max enters.

✳ SARAH: Yum! We're having gator soup, Max! Come and get it!

MAX: *(holds mouth as if feeling sick)* Argh! No, thanks. I'll just eat cornbread.

> **✳ FLUENCY TIP**
>
> Express excitement when you read Sarah's part.

Readers' Theater 3, SV 9781419031687

Comprehension

Write your answer to each question on the lines below.

1. What was your favorite part of this play?

   _____

   _____

2. What facts did you learn in this play? List at least three.

   _____

   _____

3. What is this play mostly about?

   _____

   _____

4. Describe how a bladderwort gets food.

   _____

   _____

5. List at least three things Max and Sarah saw in the Everglades.

   _____

   _____

6. Explain one example of how plants adapt to their environment.

   _____

   _____

Vocabulary

Write each vocabulary word on the line where it belongs.

> wetland   adapt   Everglades   clever   carnivorous

1. Some dogs are _____ enough to learn many tricks.

2. The spines of a cactus help it _____ to life in a hot place.

3. A(n) _____ area is covered with grass and water.

4. Many interesting plants and animals live in the _____.

5. Plants and animals that eat meat are _____.

Extension

1. With a partner, discuss what you think the main idea is and why.

   Clue 1: What is the title?

   Clue 2: What words are bold?

   Main Idea: What is important to remember?

2. In a small group, make a "How Plants Adapt" chart. Use the sample to guide you. Then present your findings to the class.

HOW PLANTS ADAPT		
PLANT	CAUSE (where it lives)	EFFECT (how it survives)
Bladderwort	Lives in very watery soil	Traps meat

Plant and Gator Soup
Readers' Theater 3, SV 9781419031687

A Day at the Weather Center

Summary

"A Day at the Weather Center" is a five-character play about a class field trip to a weather forecasting center, where some students learn more than they expected!

Meet the Players

Character	Reading Level
Zack	2.7
Teacher	2.4
Alonso	2.6
Maya	0.3
Mr. Wilder	3.8

Fluency Focus
Using Punctuation

Comprehension Focus
Identifying Main Idea

Vocabulary
atmosphere
data
forecast
operator
radar
radius

Set the Stage

Teacher Read Aloud *page 45*

This selection is about the technology that has changed weather forecasting. Read the selection aloud, using punctuation as a guide to expression. Then ask students to look through the Read Aloud to find clues that two sentences are to be read in an excited voice.

Get Ready

Vocabulary *page 46*

Use this page to introduce vocabulary. Discuss the Vocabulary Think Tank question, encouraging students to share their reasoning.

Fluency and Comprehension Warm-Ups *pages 46–47*

Review these pages with students. Use the following for students who need additional help with the concepts:

- **Using Punctuation** Ending punctuation gives you clues for reading sentences. Pause when you come to the end of a sentence with a period. Raise your voice when the end of a sentence has an exclamation point. Practice these techniques as you take turns reading paragraph 1 of the Read Aloud.

- **Identifying Main Idea** An entire selection has a main idea. Often, so does each paragraph within the selection. Look at paragraph 3 of the Read Aloud. Find and read aloud the sentence that describes the main idea.

Read Aloud Tip

Read the selection aloud. Next, introduce the fluency focus of **using punctuation**. Then reread paragraph 3 of the Read Aloud, focusing on pausing at each period. Read the paragraph again. This time, ask students to listen and note how many sentences they hear by keeping a tally of the sentences on a piece of scratch paper.

A Day at the Weather Center *pages 48–54*

Independent Practice

Set up the groups and assign each student a part. Then have students read through their assigned parts once before small group practice begins.

Small Group Practice

Assemble the groups. You may want to use the following rehearsal schedule. Each rehearsal, which should involve a complete oral read-through, has an activity to guide students.

1. First Rehearsal: Direct students' attention to the *Scene 1* label at the beginning of the play. Explain that a scene is a part of a play. Encourage students to identify the number of scenes and where each takes place. Then have them read together for the first time.

2. Vocabulary Rehearsal: Invite students to locate the vocabulary words used in the play. As students locate each word, ask them to read in unison the sentence that includes that word. Challenge volunteers to use the words in sentences that explain the words' meaning, such as: *"Forecast* means to tell what the weather will be."

3. Fluency Rehearsal: Using Punctuation Before this rehearsal, have students alternate reading aloud the Fluency Tips. Encourage them to keep these tips in mind as they read. After reading, challenge students to locate one of their lines in which a dash could be substituted for a comma. Have them each copy the line using a dash and then read it aloud to the group.

4. Comprehension Rehearsal: Identifying Main Idea During this rehearsal, have students stop at the end of Scene 1 and work together to write one sentence that identifies the main idea of the scene. Have them do the same at the end of scenes 2 and 3. You may also want to challenge groups to write one sentence that describes the main idea of the entire play.

5. Final Rehearsal: Observe this rehearsal, focusing on students' use of punctuation. For example, when Zack says, "So what's the point? Can we go now?" does the student's voice rise at the end of each question? When needed, model proper expression for students having difficulty.

Performance

This is your opportunity to sit back, relax, and enjoy the performance. Encourage students to have fun while performing!

Curtain Call *pages 55–56*

Assign these questions and activities for students to complete in a group or independently.

Vocabulary Tip

For more vocabulary practice, have students discuss the following:

- What is something that you might see or feel in Earth's **atmosphere**?

- List two ways **data** is communicated to you at home or at school.

- Do bicycle riders use **radar**? Do airplane pilots? Why or why not?

A Day at the Weather Center

Set the Stage
Teacher Read Aloud

Before the sixteenth century, if people wanted a weather report, they looked outside. There were no instruments for checking the weather. If it was raining outside, then there was a 100 percent chance of rain!

The first U.S. weather reports were made in the late 1700s to early 1800s. It wasn't until much later that the first weather map was drawn. The U.S. Army was the first to give out regular weather reports.

The core elements in weather are temperature and air pressure. A thermometer measures temperature. A barometer measures air pressure. Neither of these tools was invented until the seventeenth century.

Once people could check the temperature and the air pressure, they needed a way to communicate the forecast. The telegraph was invented in the nineteenth century. The telegraph machine sent coded messages over wires by means of electrical impulses. This was the first way the news and forecasts could be spread.

Today, you can pick up any newspaper and find a forecast. You can hear one on the radio. You can see one on TV. You can find one on the Internet. And, you can always look outside!

In this play, you will learn more about the weather. Use the vocabulary and warm-ups to help you get ready.

Vocabulary

Read and review these vocabulary words to prepare you for reading this play. Choose a word and draw its meaning to help you remember it.

atmosphere—the air around the earth

data—facts and information

forecast—a good guess of what's going to happen in the weather

operator—someone who runs something

radar—a tool that uses radio waves to figure out where something is and how fast it is going

radius—distance from the very middle of a circle to the outside rim

> ### VOCABULARY THINK TANK
>
> *Fore* in *forecast* means "before." How does this help you understand *forecast*?

Fluency Warm-Up

Using Punctuation

Fluent readers pay attention to **punctuation**. They use the punctuation as a guide to how they read. Paying attention to punctuation tells you when to pause, when to stop, when to raise or lower your voice, and when to read with emotion and excitement.

When you get to a punctuation mark, don't skip it and race forward. Stop at periods. Pause at commas. Use your question voice at a question mark. Express excitement at an exclamation point.

FLUENCY PRACTICE

Read the following paragraph. Punctuate it. Then read it again, using the punctuation to help you read fluently.

My friend came over today He's so much fun to play with We had a good time until we got into a fight I never want him to come over again He really made me mad My mom says I have to apologize to him Do you think I should

Comprehension Warm-Up

Identifying Main Idea

When you identify the **main idea** in a text, you find what is most important. Sometimes writers state the main idea directly. When writers don't state the main idea directly, you have to find clues in the text.

The title is sometimes a clue. Pictures are clues. Bold words are clues to important words. Reading is a little like being a detective.

COMPREHENSION TIP

Look for the clues to help you find the main idea.

Clue 1: What is the title?

Clue 2: What's in the pictures?

Clue 3: What words are bold?

Clue 4: What is important to remember?

47

Readers' Theater

Presents

A Day at the Weather Center

by
Judy Kentor Schmauss

Cast

(in order of appearance)

Zack   _____

Teacher   _____

Alonso   _____

Maya   _____

Mr. Wilder   _____

SCENE 1: IN THE CLASSROOM

ZACK: Another field trip. Do we have to go?

TEACHER: Yes, we've had this trip planned for a long time. Why don't you want to go?

ALONSO: You know Zack. He doesn't want to do anything.

TEACHER: Well, this field trip will be fun. You'll see how weather is tracked and **forecasted**.

MAYA: Well, I want to see how they know when tornadoes are coming. They scare me.

ZACK: There's nothing scary about it. When the weather conditions are right, you get a tornado. Same for rain, snow, hurricanes, and everything else that gets tossed at us.

ALONSO: Well, I think it'll be interesting.

TEACHER: Let's get on the bus and get going.

SCENE 2: AT THE WEATHER CENTER

TEACHER: This is Mr. Wilder, the **operator** of the weather center. He'll be showing us around.

MAYA: Are you the only operator?

MR. WILDER: No, it just seems that way. It's been very quiet lately because not much is happening, weatherwise.

ZACK: So what's the point? Can we go now?

MR. WILDER: *(looking at teacher)* Are you ready to start?

ALONSO: I am. What's that machine over there?

ZACK: That's a barometer. It measures the air pressure.

ALONSO: What's air pressure?

MAYA: My dad said the air pressure in our tires was low. Is it the same as that?

MR. WILDER: Something like it. The air in the **atmosphere** has weight and pushes down, just like everything else that has weight. Since the atmosphere is very big, that's a lot of weight and pressure.

ALONSO: What does air pressure have to do with the weather, anyway?

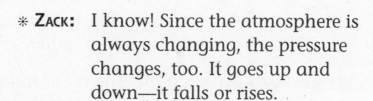

ZACK: I know! Since the atmosphere is always changing, the pressure changes, too. It goes up and down—it falls or rises.

TEACHER: Is that right, Mr. Wilder?

MR. WILDER: I can simplify it for you—if the air pressure is falling, then it means that stormy or rainy weather is coming. If the pressure rises, it means that fair weather is coming back. If the pressure stays steady, it means no big changes.

MAYA: I get it. Down means rain, up means clear. Steady means no change. That's not hard!

ALONSO: So does that mean that there's less pressure at the top of a mountain?

MR. WILDER: That's right. And where would you find the most pressure?

ZACK: At sea level, right?

MR. WILDER: Exactly. You guys are really catching on.

TEACHER: Isn't that **radar** over there? Radar tracks things like hurricanes and tornadoes—right?

❋ **FLUENCY TIP**

Look at the line in the middle of Zack's sentence. That is a dash—it means slight pause, much like a comma does.

A Day at the Weather Center
Readers' Theater 3, SV 9781419031687

ZACK: Radar can also track thunderstorms and lots of other bad weather.

✳ **MR. WILDER:** You're both right. The main radar center is in Kansas City, Missouri. Let's look on a map. Maya, can you find Kansas City?

MAYA: I think so. Wait a minute. Yes, here it is.

✳ **MR. WILDER:** Here's a 250-mile **radius** from Kansas City. I'm going to draw a circle on the map to show it to you. Alonso, what do you notice about where we live in relation to what I drew?

ALONSO: Our town is within the 250 miles!

MR. WILDER: That's right!

✳ **MAYA:** Are there only two weather centers?

MR. WILDER: No way! We're only one of hundreds of weather centers across the United States. All the centers keep track of their weather from their stations and send it out to others.

✳ **ALONSO:** So let's say you see something on the radar. When do you let everyone else know about it?

✳ **TEACHER:** Yes, how do you let the radio and television stations know what's going on?

> ✳ **FLUENCY TIP**
>
> Use your question voice when you read a question.

A Day at the Weather Center
Readers' Theater 3, SV 9781419031687

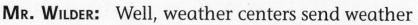

MR. WILDER: Well, weather centers send weather **data** out every hour for aviation use.

MAYA: That means for airplanes, right?

MR. WILDER: Right. The data gets sent every six hours for general forecasting.

ALONSO: That means to local weather people at TV and radio stations?

MR. WILDER: Right again.

ZACK: What kind of data is sent?

✳ **MR. WILDER:** Let's see . . . the amount of rain or snow that falls, the temperature, and the pressure. In addition, any change in wind direction and speed.

MAYA: That's a lot!

MR. WILDER: It sure is. And there are other weather centers that look for other things.

TEACHER: Excuse me, something is beeping. Is that computer supposed to beep like that?

MR. WILDER: It is when a weather system is moving through. I'm afraid I'll have to end our tour here. I hope it's been worthwhile.

> ✳ **FLUENCY TIP**
>
> Look at the ellipses (. . .) in Mr. Wilder's part. This means your voice should trail off a bit.

TEACHER: It certainly has been for me! Kids, what do you say to Mr. Wilder?

MAYA: Thanks. I'm not so scared now.

ALONSO: Thanks from me, too. It was cool!

ZACK: Yeah, thanks. It wasn't as boring as I thought it'd be. It was pretty interesting, actually. You sure we can't stay?

MR. WILDER: Not today. I've got to get going. Keep your eye on the sky . . .

SCENE 3: BACK IN THE CLASSROOM

TEACHER: Well, that was a good field trip. I, for one, am glad we went.

MAYA: I want to be a weather predictor someday!

ALONSO: It wouldn't be too shabby to work at a weather center. Lots of cool computers and stuff.

ZACK: Can we go on another field trip next week?

Comprehension

Write your answer to each question on the lines below.

1. How do weather forecasters use radar? _____

_____

2. Why are there so many weather centers across the United States?

_____

_____

3. Why do you think Mr. Wilder has to end the tour early?

_____

_____

4. What are two things you learned about forecasting the weather?

_____

_____

5. Why do you think Maya wasn't so scared of tornadoes anymore?

_____

_____

6. What was Zack like at the beginning of the play? What was he like at

the end? _____

_____

_____

7. Why is taking a field trip like this one a good idea?

_____

_____

Vocabulary

Finish the paragraph by writing a vocabulary word on each line.

operator	forecast	data	radius	atmosphere	radar

My mother is the (1) _____ of our town's weather center. Every day she uses a lot of weather machines. She checks the (2) _____ to see if any storms are headed our way. She checks to see what is happening in the (3) _____. She uses all these (4) _____ to figure out what the weather will do next. Then she makes a (5) _____ so everyone else knows, too.

Extension

1. Make a chart that compares tornadoes, hurricanes, and snowstorms. Do some research in the library or on the Internet to find more information. You can use the chart on page 10.

2. Why is knowing about the weather so important to our everyday lives? Discuss the answers to this question in small groups. Share your answers with the rest of the class. Do the activity on page 11.

A Day at the Weather Center
Readers' Theater 3, SV 9781419031687

The Fourth Rock from the Sun

Summary

"The Fourth Rock from the Sun" is a six-character play about the first child ever to visit Mars.

Meet the Players

Character	Reading Level
Narrator	2.0
Tyler	0.6
Mom	2.1
Astronaut 1	0.2
Astronaut 2	2.1
Astronaut 3	2.0

Fluency Focus
Using Expression

Comprehension Focus
Asking Questions

Vocabulary
atmosphere
craters
gravity
NASA
volcano
weightless

Read Aloud Tip

Read the selection once, and then return to it to model the fluency focus of **using expression**. Explain that readers make text more interesting by stressing key words. Reread the last sentence in paragraph 3 of the Read Aloud, emphasizing the word *your*. Invite students to suggest a word to stress in the next paragraph, and then have them read that sentence to you.

Set the Stage

Teacher Read Aloud *page 59*

This selection is about the National Aeronautics and Space Administration (NASA). Read the selection aloud. As you do, ask students to listen to how you say some words louder than others.

Get Ready

Vocabulary *page 60*

Use this page to introduce vocabulary. Discuss students' answers to the Vocabulary Think Tank question. Then ask them to work together to list five ways that gravity affects their lives.

Fluency and Comprehension Warm-Ups *pages 60–61*

Review these pages with students. Use the following for students who need additional help with the concepts:

- **Using Expression** Part of using expression is deciding what words to stress, or read with a stronger voice. Read the first sentence of the Read Aloud together, stressing these important words: *NASA, researches, explores.*

- **Asking Questions** Good readers think about what they are reading and ask questions about it. For example, after reading the Read Aloud, you may wonder how long it would take to reach Mars. Your question might be answered in the play. If not, you could do some research.

The Fourth Rock from the Sun *pages 62–68*

Independent Practice
Set up the groups and assign each student a part. Then have students read through their assigned parts once before small group practice begins.

Small Group Practice
Assemble the groups. You may want to use the following rehearsal schedule. Each rehearsal, which should involve a complete oral read-through, has an activity to guide students.

1. First Rehearsal: Have groups work together to preview the play by reading the title and looking at the illustrations. Draw their attention to lines that say *All* and explain that everyone will read those lines in unison. Then invite students to read together for the first time.

2. Vocabulary Rehearsal: Invite students to locate and list the vocabulary words used in the play. Challenge groups to work together to choose one word and create a Word Splash by writing the word at the center of a sheet of paper and surrounding it with words or ideas associated with that word.

3. Fluency Rehearsal: Using Expression Call attention to the Fluency Tip on page 63. Ask students to study Tyler's first line and to find a clue that the words should be read in an excited voice. Then challenge them to find other exclamation points on the page. Have students read Mom's lines in unison, using an excited voice.

4. Comprehension Rehearsal: Asking Questions After this rehearsal, have groups work together to create a list of at least three questions they still have about NASA, astronauts, space travel, or Mars. Allow the groups to share their lists. Provide references, and invite students to look for answers to their questions during their free time.

5. Final Rehearsal: Observe this rehearsal, focusing on students' ability to use the meaning of what they read as a clue to proper expression. For example, do students read the line "Ewww!" as if they were disgusted?

Performance
This is your opportunity to sit back, relax, and enjoy the performance. Encourage students to have fun while performing!

Curtain Call *pages 69–70*
Assign these questions and activities for students to complete in a group or independently.

Vocabulary Tip
For more vocabulary practice, have students discuss the following:

- Would you visit **NASA** to learn about trains or about rockets?
- What are some of the dangers of an erupting **volcano**?
- What makes up the **atmosphere**?

The Fourth Rock from the Sun
Readers' Theater 3, SV 9781419031687

The Fourth Rock from the Sun

Set the Stage
Teacher Read Aloud

NASA is a government agency that researches and explores space. The agency's full name is the National Aeronautics and Space Administration. NASA was created in 1958, mostly because the Soviet Union launched a spaceship in 1957 called *Sputnik*. Not wanting to be outdone, the United States started its own agency and missions.

One of NASA's goals was to send humans to the moon. In 1969, the U.S. astronaut Neil Armstrong was the first person to walk on the moon.

The NASA space program has been studying Mars for many years. In 2004, NASA landed an unmanned exploration rover on Mars. NASA plans to launch additional spacecraft to study Mars. Future Mars missions will study good landing sites for possible human visits. Maybe in your lifetime, humans will make the long journey to Mars.

In this play, you will learn more about NASA and the planets Mars and Saturn. Use the vocabulary and warm-ups to help you get ready.

www.harcourtschoolsupply.com
59
The Fourth Rock from the Sun
Readers' Theater 3, SV 9781419031687

Get Ready

Vocabulary

Read and review these vocabulary words to prepare you for reading this play. Say each word aloud two times.

atmosphere (AT mus fear)—the gases that surround a planet

craters—bowl-shaped holes in a planet or moon

gravity—natural force that gives objects weight

NASA—the National Aeronautics and Space Administration

volcano (vahl KAY no)—a cone shaped mountain that spits steam, ash, fire, and rocks

weightless—free from gravity

VOCABULARY THINK TANK

What would happen at the bus stop if there were no gravity?

Fluency Warm-Up

Using Expression

When you use **expression**, you use your voice to bring out the meaning and feeling of the words.

How will you know what to express? First, watch out for punctuation. For example, an exclamation point can tell you when to read with anger or excitement. Second, try to imagine what the writer or a character may be thinking or feeling.

FLUENCY PRACTICE

1. Read this with an angry voice. I found my homework.
2. Read this with a happy voice. I found my homework.
3. How would you read this? THAT'S MY HOMEWORK!
4. How would you read this? That's my homework?

Comprehension Warm-Up

Asking Questions

Good readers pause to **ask questions**. Then they search for the answers.

As you read, keep track of the questions you ask. Try using self-stick notes or a journal. Then make sure to find those answers!

COMPREHENSION TIP

Stop and ask yourself questions like these as you read.

1. Is the title a clue?
2. Do any words look important?
3. What do the pictures tell me?
4. What is the purpose of this story?

Readers' Theater

Presents

The Fourth Rock from the Sun

by
Laura Layton Strom

Cast
(in order of appearance)

Narrator   _____

Tyler   _____

Mom   _____

Astronaut 1   _____

Astronaut 2   _____

Astronaut 3   _____

NARRATOR: The year is 2026. A space station has been built on Mars. Spaceships are sent from Earth every two years. They are sent when Mars and Earth are closest. A space camp contest was held, and now the winner is the first child to fly to Mars.

＊ **TYLER:** I am on a spaceship to Mars! And I am only 9 years old!

MOM: You would be 4 years old on Mars. And I would be 18! There are 687 days in a year on Mars. There are 365 days in a year on Earth.

TYLER: Mom, you are so good at math! How much will I weigh on Mars?

MOM: That is easy. You multiply your Earth weight by 0.38. So you will weigh 30 pounds. I will weigh 46!

TYLER: It is so strange to be in outer space. I want to laugh for no reason. My head is stuffy, too. My eyes feel like they might pop out.

ASTRONAUT 1: That is OK, Tyler. We get those strange feelings, too. You will get used to feeling strange. It will take a few days.

＊ **FLUENCY TIP**

Remember to express excitement when you read Tyler's first lines.

TYLER: It will take us 260 days to get to Mars. That is 8 months! But it will be worth it. The sun is setting, so I'm going to cross off Day One.

ASTRONAUT 2: You can't chart by sunrise and sunset, Tyler.

MOM: You can keep track of Earth days on your watch. Are you wearing the watch **NASA** gave you?

TYLER: Yes, Mom. I have it on. So what are we going to do for fun up here?

ASTRONAUT 1: I know a fun game. I will throw a peanut into the air. You float through the air and catch it. Don't use your hands. You have to eat it like a fish.

ASTRONAUT 3: There is no **gravity**. Being **weightless** can be fun. I like to float. Let's show him how the peanut game works. *(Astronaut 1 tosses a peanut. Astronaut 3 acts like a fish trying to eat it.)*

ASTRONAUT 2: Looking out the window is fun. Look at the Earth right now. See that dark spot right there. *(Pointing.)* That is the Grand Canyon.

The Fourth Rock from the Sun
Readers' Theater 3, SV 9781419031687

TYLER: In our training, we learned that we will see an even bigger canyon on Mars. And there is a **volcano** on Mars that is three times taller than the tallest mountain on Earth!

MOM: Anyone want some food?

TYLER: Sure, what are we having? I could go for a hamburger and fries.

ASTRONAUT 2: How about spaghetti, dried apricots, and chocolate pudding?

＊ **ALL:** Yum!

ASTRONAUT 1: You must be careful when you eat. Bits of food can float around the spaceship. Drink spills turn into blobs. Flying bits and blobs are not fun.

ASTRONAUT 3: Yes, once I breathed in some food crumbs. I think I breathed in a toenail clipping once, too. Zero gravity is tricky.

＊ **ALL:** Ewww!

＊ **FLUENCY TIP**

On the lines for "ALL," make sure you read those lines with excitement. They have exclamation points.

The Fourth Rock from the Sun
Readers' Theater 3, SV 9781419031687

Mom: Well, we will be very careful not to spill things.

Narrator: The *Mars Scout 9* is now nearing touchdown on Mars. The two moons look like giant potatoes. Mars is light red and has **craters**.

Tyler: It sure looks like Mars has rivers. Look at all those lines.

Astronaut 2: Some scientists think Mars had water in the past.

Astronaut 3: In fact, some scientists think there might be water below the surface.

Astronaut 1: There are many scientists at the space station. They are doing tests. The teams are looking for water and maybe signs of life.

Astronaut 2: There is also a team studying the **atmosphere**. They might be able to add gases to it. Then they could make Mars more like Earth.

Astronaut 3: Another team is studying melting the polar ice caps. This would create oceans.

Mom: Some scientists are trying to make Mars warmer. They might try putting mirrors in space.

TYLER: Mars is pretty cold. Sometimes the surface is warm. But the atmosphere is often below freezing. WAY below freezing. Brr!

ASTRONAUT 1: But you will be warm in the space station.

MOM: I am looking forward to exploring Mars.

TYLER: I'm ready! Are we there yet?

NARRATOR: The *Mars Scout 9* lander makes a soft landing on Mars. The surface looks like a rocky desert. Tyler hears the crunch of Mars dust under his shoes. He smiles. His dream has come true.

TYLER: Wow! The space station is huge! It is so much bigger than the pictures I saw.

MOM: Yes, it is really beautiful. What are those green things against the glass?

TYLER: Maybe they are Martians!

ASTRONAUT 3: Ha! Unfortunately, no. Those are plants. We have a farm in there where we grow fruits and vegetables. You see banana trees.

www.harcourtschoolsupply.com
67
The Fourth Rock from the Sun
Readers' Theater 3, SV 9781419031687

Mom: I can't believe we are really walking on Mars. Do you realize YOU are making history, Tyler? You are the first child to ever walk on Mars!

Tyler: I am! I am! I really am! May I take a rock home? I promised my teacher a rock from Mars.

Astronaut 1: I suppose that would be OK. Looks like Mars can spare it. There is a nice rock by that crater.

Tyler: *(picks up the rock and looks at it)* Hey, look at this! *(Shows it around.)* It looks like there are tiny bones in this rock.

✳ **Astronaut 3:** Let me see that. Oh, my! That looks like a fossil. We need to get this to the lab, Tyler. This may be another first for humankind. This may be proof of earlier life on Mars!

(All join hands and jump up and down.)

✳ **FLUENCY TIP**

Astronaut 3 is surprised and excited at the end. Use your voice to express his feelings.

Comprehension

Write your answer to each question on the lines below.

1. Why do spaceships travel to Mars only every two years?

_____

_____

2. What is one good thing about being weightless? What is one bad thing?

_____

_____

3. What are three ways that Mars is different from Earth?

_____

_____

4. Why do you think the astronauts grow plants in the space station?

_____

_____

5. What was your favorite part of this play? Why?

_____

_____

6. List three facts that you learned from this play.

_____

_____

7. Do you think it is possible that people will visit Mars someday? Why?

_____

_____

Vocabulary

Write the number of a vocabulary word on the line before its meaning.

1. volcano   _____ Layers of air around Earth

2. craters   _____ Without weight

3. gravity   _____ Mountain that erupts with gases and lava

4. atmosphere   _____ Force that pulls objects toward Earth

5. weightless   _____ Group that includes astronauts

6. NASA   _____ Large, shallow holes on the surface of land

Extension

1. Would you want to be the first child to visit Mars? In small groups, make a Pros and Cons Chart. Then share your ideas with the class.

SAMPLE: THE FIRST CHILD TO VISIT MARS	
PROS	CONS
I would be famous.	I would miss my friends.

2. With a small group, go to the NASA Web site at www.nasa.gov.

   - Find out what space missions are planned.

   - Do a short report explaining a few of these plans.

   - Then read aloud the report to the class.

The Fourth Rock from the Sun
Readers' Theater 3, SV 9781419031687

The Worst Thanksgiving Ever

Summary

"The Worst Thanksgiving Ever" is a six-character play about a family whose Thanksgiving celebration looks bleak when a storm knocks out the electricity—and keeps Dad from getting home.

Meet the Players

Character	Reading Level
Narrator	5.8
Mom	2.8
Millie	1.9
Grandpa	2.8
Grandma	4.6
Eddy	1.7

Fluency Focus
Reading with Word Accuracy

Comprehension Focus
Building Background

Vocabulary
celebration
harvest
inedible
Pilgrims
spices
tradition

Set the Stage

Teacher Read Aloud *page 73*
This selection is about traditional Thanksgiving celebrations in different cultures and times. Read the selection aloud. As you do, model good fluency, asking students to listen for multisyllabic words.

Get Ready

Vocabulary *page 74*
Use this page to introduce vocabulary. Discuss the Vocabulary Think Tank question. Then have students compose a sentence about a family tradition and read it aloud to a partner.

Fluency and Comprehension Warm-Ups *pages 74–75*
Review these pages with students. Use the following for students who need additional help with the concepts:

- **Reading with Word Accuracy** When you come to unfamiliar words, remember to look for parts of the word that you know. Put the parts together to say a word that makes sense. Then practice saying the word. Try doing this with words from the Read Aloud, such as *celebration*.

- **Building Background** Thinking about what you already know about a topic helps you understand what you read. List five things you already know about Thanksgiving. Underline one fact that helps you understand what the Read Aloud is about.

Read Aloud Tip

Introduce the fluency focus of **reading with word accuracy**. Write *centuries* and *festivals* on the board. Point out that before reading aloud, good readers think about how to pronounce difficult words. They look at each part of the word and then put the parts together. Have students read each word with you, first stressing the separate syllables and then reading the word as a whole.

71

The Worst Thanksgiving Ever pages 76–82

Independent Practice

Set up the groups and assign each student a part. Then have students read through their assigned parts once before small group practice begins.

Small Group Practice

Assemble the groups. You may want to use the following rehearsal schedule. Each rehearsal, which should involve a complete oral read-through, has an activity to guide students.

1. First Rehearsal: Guide students through a play preview by reading the title, character list, and stage directions. Invite volunteers to make some predictions related to the title "The Worst Thanksgiving Ever." Then invite students to read together as a group.

2. Vocabulary Rehearsal: Direct students to locate and list the vocabulary words used in the play. Then have students work together to find and discuss two vocabulary words that are related in some way. For example, students could discuss how a *celebration* is a way of carrying on *traditions*.

3. Fluency Rehearsal: Reading with Word Accuracy Draw students' attention to the word *Thanksgiving*. Point out that it is a compound word—a word made up of two smaller words. To read the word, pronounce both small words and blend them together. Have students locate and read aloud five additional compound words on page 78. *(thunderstorm, houseboat, anywhere, without, inside)*

4. Comprehension Rehearsal: Building Background
Have students brainstorm a list of things they already know about thunderstorms. After the rehearsal, have groups refer to the list and to the play to create thunderstorm word webs that tell how a thunderstorm looks, sounds, and feels. Use the blackline master on page 13.

5. Final Rehearsal: Observe this rehearsal, focusing on students' ability to read with word accuracy. As a student reads his or her dialogue, note any mispronunciations. Use this information to provide help to individual students.

Performance

This is your opportunity to sit back, relax, and enjoy the performance. Encourage students to have fun while performing!

Curtain Call pages 83–84

Assign these questions and activities for students to complete in a group or independently.

Vocabulary Tip

For more vocabulary practice, have students discuss the following:

- List or draw three things you could **harvest**.

- Tell which of these things are **inedible**: chocolate, an apple, coal, peanuts, mud.

- If you do something for the first time, is it a **tradition**? Why or why not?

The Worst Thanksgiving Ever

Set the Stage
Teacher Read Aloud

All through history, people have set aside days for giving thanks.

Thousands of years ago, both the ancient Greeks and Romans had feasts in the fall to give thanks for a year of good crops.

For centuries, the Chinese have had similar festivals. Their thanksgiving celebration centers on the moon. Each year they bake special moon-shaped cakes. These cakes are eaten over the three days that they give thanks for their harvest.

Even the ancient Egyptians had thanksgiving celebrations. But they held theirs in the springtime because that is when they gathered their crops.

In the United States, the tradition of celebrating Thanksgiving goes back almost four hundred years. In this play, you will learn more about what makes Thanksgiving such a special holiday. Use the vocabulary words and warm-ups to help you get ready.

Vocabulary

Read and review these vocabulary words to prepare you for reading this play. Draw a picture that will remind you what each word means.

celebration—an activity or party to honor a special occasion

harvest—the gathering of a crop, or the time of year a crop is gathered

inedible—not fit to be eaten

Pilgrims—English colonists who founded the first permanent settlement in New England

spices—plant products used to flavor foods

tradition—the handing down of stories, beliefs, or customs from parents to children

> ### VOCABULARY THINK TANK
>
> What is one of your family's Thanksgiving traditions?

Fluency Warm-Up

Reading with Word Accuracy

Fluent readers pay attention to the parts of a word so that they read smoothly and with **accuracy**. You will need to put the sounds of the parts together and then see if the word makes sense.

Remember to look for letters that blend or make one sound. Make sure it makes sense.

> ### FLUENCY PRACTICE
>
> What parts are alike in these words?
>
> | | | | |
> |---|---|---|---|
> | 1. | harp | harvest | harsh |
> | 2. | special | spices | spent |
> | 3. | action | celebration | creation |

Comprehension Warm-Up

Building Background

Building background will help you better understand the story. To build background knowledge, think about what you already know about a topic.

If you don't know much about a topic, research the topic to learn more. Think about what you need to know.

COMPREHENSION TIP

As you read, ask yourself questions like these.

1. How much do I know about this topic?

2. Have I heard a similar story before?

3. What would I like to learn about this topic?

Readers' Theater

Presents

The Worst Thanksgiving Ever

by
Natalie West

Cast
(in order of appearance)

Narrator _____

Mom _____

Millie _____

Grandpa _____

Grandma _____

Eddy _____

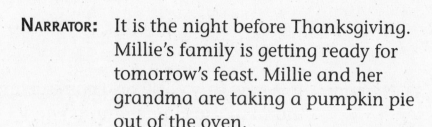

Narrator: It is the night before Thanksgiving. Millie's family is getting ready for tomorrow's feast. Millie and her grandma are taking a pumpkin pie out of the oven.

Mom: I wish I hadn't fallen and broken my leg. *(Points to leg.)* Now I can't help make Thanksgiving dinner.

Millie: Don't worry, Mom. Grandma, Eddy, and I can cook. I bet even Grandpa will help.

Grandpa: I don't think you want my help in the kitchen if you actually want to eat the food. Everything I make is **inedible**. *(Everyone laughs.)*

Grandma: You are so right! Remember when you made tuna surprise and forgot the tuna? I was sure surprised!

Eddy: That's OK, Gramps—you have other talents. Besides, Dad will be home tomorrow. He loves to cook.

Grandma: Someone on the radio said another big thunderstorm is on the way. I hope your dad makes it here before the storm hits.

Millie: More rain? I can't believe it!

GRANDPA: I'm starting to think we should buy a houseboat!

✳ NARRATOR: It is now very early on Thanksgiving morning. Flashing lightning and booming thunder wake the entire family.

GRANDPA: I can barely see across the street! This is the worst thunderstorm I've seen in years!

EDDY: What if the roads flood? How will Dad get home?

MOM: I don't know. If this storm continues, it's going to be hard to get anywhere.

MILLIE: This will be the WORST Thanksgiving ever, if Dad can't get home!

EDDY: Yeah, who's going to carve the turkey? Dad always carves the turkey. It's a family **tradition**. Thanksgiving won't be Thanksgiving without Dad.

GRANDMA: Well, let's be thankful that we're all nice and dry inside.

GRANDPA: And let's think positive thoughts about your dad getting home today.

✳ FLUENCY TIP

Notice words with similar endings, such as *morning, lightning,* and *booming.* Find the root word in each. This will help you read a long word correctly.

MILLIE: If I think he'll be home today, will it happen?

GRANDMA: A negative attitude never helps anyone. Now, who's going to help me stuff this bird? *(Pointing to the turkey.)*

NARRATOR: Eddy, Millie, and even Grandpa help Grandma stuff the turkey. Grandma sprinkles the stuffing with **spices** and pops the turkey into the oven.

NARRATOR: Just then, the telephone rings, and Eddy gets it.

EDDY: Hi, Dad! Happy Thanksgiving! Where are you? When will you be home? *(He waits for an answer, frowns, and hangs up.)*

EDDY: Dad said it's storming where he is, too. He doesn't know when he'll be home.

MILLIE: No! This is the worst Thanksgiving ever!

MOM: What happened to positive thinking? Dad is safe, and the five of us are together.

NARRATOR: It's late afternoon, and the smell of the turkey is making everyone's mouth water. Grandma asks Eddy and Millie to help peel potatoes.

GRANDPA: *(entering the kitchen)* It smells great in here! Do you need my help?

✳ GRANDMA: I think my two helpers *(pointing at Millie and Eddy)* and I have it under control. Besides, you said it yourself— anything you cook is inedible!

GRANDPA: You're right. I am the world's worst cook. So, instead of ruining the food, I'll start a fire in the fireplace.

EDDY: *(eager to get out of peeling potatoes)* That's a great idea, Gramps. I'll help you get some wood.

MOM: *(slicing vegetables)* Eddy, please put on your rain jacket.

GRANDPA: It's really windy, too. I hope we don't lose our electricity.

NARRATOR: Just as Grandpa finishes speaking, the lights begin to flicker. Then they go out completely.

MILLIE: I think you spoke too soon, Grandpa.

GRANDMA: Oh, dear! We can't finish cooking dinner now!

GRANDPA: At least the turkey's done.

> **✳ FLUENCY TIP**
>
> When you come to a new word, break it into pieces and try reading it again. *In-ed-i-ble*

NARRATOR: A few hours later, the electricity is still out. The fire that Eddy and Grandpa built has made the house toasty. The flickering candles add a warm glow. But no one is feeling very thankful— especially Millie.

MILLIE: This is really, truly the worst Thanksgiving ever! We have no lights, no food, and no Dad.

MOM: Don't give up on Thanksgiving just yet. I have an idea that might be a lot of fun. We're going to pretend we're the **Pilgrims**!

EDDY: How are we going to do that, Mom? Dress up in funny clothes and hats?

MOM: No, we're going to have our own **harvest**. We're going to gather whatever foods we can. Then we'll make a wonderful feast.

MILLIE: Is that what the Pilgrims did? I thought they ate corn on Thanksgiving.

EDDY: Yes, they ate corn, peas, and other things. But we have no electricity to cook. How can we have any Thanksgiving foods?

GRANDMA: At the Pilgrims first thanksgiving **celebration**, they ate foods that were available to them. They didn't eat the traditional Thanksgiving foods that we have today.

EDDY: So, by not eating the traditional Thanksgiving foods, we're being more like the Pilgrims?

MOM: Exactly! Now, let's all get to work and see what we can harvest.

NARRATOR: Eddy finds popcorn to pop. Grandpa gets hotdogs to roast. Grandma finds potato chips. Millie gets marshmallows.

GRANDMA: *(smiling at her family)* I think we sometimes forget the true meaning of Thanksgiving. It's about spending time with people you care about. And it's about giving thanks for them. It's not about eating a lot of food.

EDDY: *(standing at the window)* Look! It stopped raining! And, hey, there's a car.

MILLIE: This is the best Thanksgiving ever!

Comprehension

Write your answer to each question on the lines below.

1. Name three ways that this Thanksgiving is different from the family's

   traditional celebration. _____

   _____

2. What does it mean when the narrator says "the smell of the turkey is

   making everyone's mouth water"? _____

   _____

3. Why does Eddy want to help Grandpa get wood?

   _____

   _____

4. How does losing the electricity cause problems?

   _____

   _____

5. What was your favorite part of this play? Why?

   _____

   _____

6. Why was this "the best Thanksgiving ever"?

   _____

   _____

7. Did you ever have to change plans because of bad weather? Tell about it.

   _____

   _____

Readers' Theater 3, SV 9781419031687

Vocabulary

Write the number of a vocabulary word on the line before its meaning.

1. harvest   _____ Not good to eat

2. spices   _____ Something done for many years

3. celebration   _____ Group of people who settled in America

4. inedible   _____ Party

5. tradition   _____ Flavorings, such as salt and pepper

6. Pilgrims   _____ To pick crops

Extension

1. With a partner, research the first Thanksgiving. Answer the following questions.

   • Who did the Pilgrims invite to their feast?

   • What were the Pilgrims thankful for?

2. In a small group, imagine that you are chefs who are preparing the best feast in the world. Make a poster for the feast. Detail what you will serve.

The Tallest Tale Ever

Summary

"The Tallest Tale Ever" is a six-character play about an amazing rescue during the Sugar Creek Storytelling Festival.

Meet the Players

Character	Reading Level
Narrator	5.4
Miss Fishpenny	4.3
Ava	2.8
Leo	2.6
Kate	2.3
Nic	3.1

Fluency Focus
Phrasing Properly

Comprehension Focus
Summarizing

Vocabulary
brilliant
entertain
exaggerate
humorous
unbelievable

Read Aloud Tip

Use the Read Aloud to practice the fluency focus of **phrasing properly**. Copy the first sentence onto the board. Draw lines to indicate word chunks that would result in improper phrasing. Read the sentence aloud, using the incorrect phrasing. Then erase the lines and draw new lines to chunk the words properly. Invite students to read the properly phrased sentence with you.

Set the Stage

Teacher Read Aloud *page 87*

This selection is about the legend of Paul Bunyan. Read the selection aloud. Ask students to follow along, noting commas in the text and how you group words that come before and after each comma.

Get Ready

Vocabulary *page 88*

Use this page to introduce vocabulary. Discuss the Vocabulary Think Tank question, asking students to explain their choices.

Fluency and Comprehension Warm-Ups *pages 88–89*

Review these pages with students. Use the following for students who need additional help with the concepts:

• **Phrasing Properly** Think about the meaning of what you read. Remember to chunk words into phrases that make sense. For example, in the first sentence of paragraph 4 of the Read Aloud, it makes sense to chunk the words *Paul got a pet blue ox named Babe—on his first birthday.* A chunk like *Paul got a pet—blue ox named Babe—on his first birthday* doesn't make sense. Take turns reading other sentences from the Read Aloud.

• **Summarizing** As you read, think about the characters and what happens to them. For example, turn to the Read Aloud and look at paragraph 2. Write one sentence that tells what you learned about Paul Bunyan in this paragraph.

The Tallest Tale Ever *pages 90–96*

Independent Practice

Set up the groups and assign each student a part. Then have students read through their assigned parts once before small group practice begins.

Small Group Practice

Assemble the groups. You may want to use the following rehearsal schedule. Each rehearsal, which should involve a complete oral read-through, has an activity to guide students.

1. First Rehearsal: Ask students to preview the play by reading the title, character list, and stage directions. Students should then read the play together as a group for the first time.

2. Vocabulary Rehearsal: After this rehearsal, review the definition of *exaggerate* on page 88. Ask students to fold a sheet of paper in half. Then have each student choose one exaggeration from the play and draw the scene on half of the paper. On the other half, have them draw the same scene as it probably really happened. Encourage students to share their drawings with the group.

3. Fluency Rehearsal: Phrasing Properly Before this rehearsal, encourage students to review the Fluency Tips. After the rehearsal, invite them to choose one of their lines and to read it aloud in the group, stressing the most important words. Challenge students who are listening to identify the stressed words.

4. Comprehension Rehearsal: Summarizing After this rehearsal, have students work together in groups to complete the Story Map on page 12. Then challenge groups to use the Story Map as a guide for writing a four- or five-sentence summary of the play.

5. Final Rehearsal: Observe this rehearsal, focusing on students' ability to phrase properly. For example, Ava's second line on page 91 should be phrased as follows: *You always exaggerate,—Leo.—If it had rained that much,—the whole world would be flooded.*

Performance

This is your opportunity to sit back, relax, and enjoy the performance. Encourage students to have fun while performing!

Curtain Call *pages 97–98*

Assign these questions and activities for students to complete in a group or independently.

Vocabulary Tip

For more vocabulary practice, have students discuss the following:

- Is anything that happens in this play **unbelievable**?

- How can both the sun and a student be **brilliant**?

- Can words be **humorous**? Can pictures?

The Tallest Tale Ever

Set the Stage

Teacher Read Aloud

One of the most famous tall tales of all time is the story of Paul Bunyan.

Paul Bunyan was a giant lumberjack. He was even a giant when he was born. It took five giant storks to deliver him to his mother and father.

He grew so fast that after one week he was wearing his father's clothes. But he grew more, and soon he used wagon wheels for his buttons. He could eat 40 bowls of porridge before he even started his meal.

Paul got a pet blue ox named Babe on his first birthday. Babe grew very large as well. Paul and Babe were so large that their footsteps formed the 10,000 lakes in Minnesota.

In this play, you will read about this "larger-than-life" hero, Paul Bunyan. Use the vocabulary words and warm-ups to help you get ready.

Vocabulary

Read and review these vocabulary words to prepare you for reading this play. Which of these words are adjectives, or describing words?

brilliant—bright; smart; shining

entertain—to amuse

exaggerate—to make something seem larger or greater

humorous—funny

unbelievable—very hard to believe

> **VOCABULARY THINK TANK**
>
> Would you rather be brilliant or humorous? Why?

Fluency Warm-Up

Phrasing Properly

Fluent readers read in chunks, or **phrases**. Reading word-for-word not only sounds dull, it breaks down the meaning of the sentence. Meaning comes from phrases, not individual words.

There are times when punctuation will help you phrase correctly. However, sometimes you will have to figure out phrasing on your own. Listen to which words you are stressing. If a sentence doesn't make sense, try reading it another way.

> **FLUENCY PRACTICE**
>
> Chunk this sentence into two or three groups. Rewrite it, putting a slash (/) in between each group.
>
> Patty helped clear the table and wash the dishes.

Comprehension Warm-Up

Summarizing

Summarizing means retelling the important parts of a story. You can tell about the characters and what happened.

Write your answers down on a separate sheet of paper as you read. Now you have notes for your summary!

COMPREHENSION TIP

Answers to these questions will help you summarize.

1. What does the title tell me?
2. What is the main problem or conflict?
3. How is the problem solved at the end?

Readers' Theater

Presents

The Tallest Tale Ever

by
Loretta West

Cast

(in order of appearance)

Narrator   _____

Miss Fishpenny   _____

Ava   _____

Leo   _____

Kate   _____

Nic   _____

NARRATOR: Miss Fishpenny, Sugar Creek School's librarian, is standing near a window in the school library. Her eyes are filling with tears as she looks at the pouring rain. Third graders are in the library.

MISS FISHPENNY: *(blowing her nose)* For the first time in thirty years, we will have to cancel Sugar Creek's Storytelling Festival. It's too, too wet.

AVA: Oh, no! We can't call off the festival. The whole town comes to sit around campfires and listen to the stories.

LEO: Well, it's going to be pretty hard to keep the campfires lit in this rain. I bet it's already rained a hundred feet.

AVA: You always **exaggerate**, Leo. If it had rained that much, the whole world would be flooded.

KATE: I have an idea.

MISS FISHPENNY: What is your idea, Kate?

KATE: Well . . . it's not too wet INSIDE. Why don't we move the outdoor storytelling festival indoors!

The Tallest Tale Ever
Readers' Theater 3, SV 9781419031687

AVA: I love it! We can cover the library's walls with large sheets of paper and then paint forest scenes.

LEO: And we can hang lanterns and strings of lights all around the library.

MISS FISHPENNY: People can sit on the floor in small groups, and every thirty minutes I'll blow a whistle. Each group will then move to another storyteller.

NIC: I hate to admit it, but Kate's idea is pretty **brilliant**.

NARRATOR: By the next evening, the school's library has been changed into a tree-filled forest. The forest includes all sorts of animals, too—stuffed, of course. From the ceiling, tiny lights twinkle like stars. Miss Fishpenny blows a whistle, and the room grows quiet.

MISS FISHPENNY: Welcome to Sugar Creek School's 31st Storytelling Festival. You'll hear a new story every thirty minutes. Let the storytelling begin!

AVA: *(turning to talk to Kate)* I'm going to the tall tales storyteller first. Tall tales are so **humorous**.

> **FLUENCY TIP**
>
> Remember to read phrases, and not word-for-word.

Readers' Theater 3, SV 9781419031687

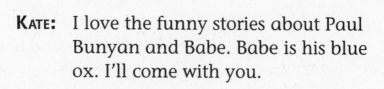

KATE: I love the funny stories about Paul Bunyan and Babe. Babe is his blue ox. I'll come with you.

LEO: Me, too. Maybe we'll hear the story about the "year of the two winters."

AVA: Is that the story about the time the snow was so deep that Paul Bunyan had to dig *down* to cut the trees?

LEO: Yep, and the trees were billions of feet tall, so the snow must have been zillions of feet high!

AVA: Are you trying to tell the tallest tale ever, Leo? Even the storytellers don't exaggerate that much.

NIC: You guys are crazy. Tall tales are too **unbelievable** for me. Give me a good science fiction story anytime.

KATE: You say tall tales are UN-believable. But you think little green people ARE believable?

NIC: I'd rather run into a little green man than an overweight blue cow any day.

KATE: Babe's a blue ox—not a cow.

The Tallest Tale Ever
Readers' Theater 3, SV 9781419031687

NARRATOR: The storytellers keep their audiences so **entertained** that no one bothers to look out a window. It isn't raining any longer, but it sure is getting nasty out there.

LEO: *(looking out a window and pointing)* Look at the snow. It must have snowed at least three feet!

MISS FISHPENNY: Leo, how many times have I asked you not to exaggerate?

AVA: *(laughing)* You've told him at least a million times.

NIC: Wow! This time he's not exaggerating. The snow is up to the window's ledge. It's a swirling blizzard.

MISS FISHPENNY: Oh, dear. How could it have snowed so much in such a short time? It just isn't possible.

KATE: It snowed more than this the "year of the two winters."

NIC: We all know that the "year of the two winters" never happened—it's part of a tall tale.

FLUENCY TIP

Reread any sentences that do not make sense.

Miss Fishpenny: We also know that many tall tales were based on things that actually happened and were about people who actually lived. Tall tales are often exaggerated history.

Narrator: More snow falls. Suddenly, the lights flicker twice and then go out. A horrible creaking sound comes from above. Everyone realizes that the heavy snow could cause the roof to fall in.

Miss Fishpenny: Please don't panic. I'm sure the roof is just fine . . . and the snow will stop soon.

Kate: Did you hear that? Someone is outside—I hear talking.

Ava: I think I heard someone say, "Pull harder, Babe."

Nic: Right, and I hear little green men shoveling off the roof.

Miss Fishpenny: Children, I know we are all worried, but this is no time for imaginations to go wild.

Leo: *(pointing out a window)* Wow! There are two giants outside. One of them is holding the biggest shovel I've ever seen.

KATE: *(looking out the window)* The other one is a blue ox, and it's pulling a big sled full of snow.

MISS FISHPENNY: It just can't be . . . can it?

KATE: It can, and it is!

NIC: It's . . . Paul Bunyan and Babe! This is unbelievable.

LEO: They got the snow off the roof. Paul Bunyan and Babe saved our lives. I won't ever have to exaggerate again—this is the greatest and tallest tale ever!

AVA: *(pointing)* Nic, look. It's a little green man.

NIC: Where? I don't see a little green man.

AVA: *(laughing)* Just kidding.

NARRATOR: No one in Sugar Creek will ever forget what happened tonight. The tale about how Paul Bunyan and Babe saved everyone in Sugar Creek will be told and retold for years to come.

KATE: Well, Nic, what do you think about tall tales now?

NIC: I think I'd rather listen to one than be in one.

FLUENCY TIP

Listen to which words you are stressing. Make sure to stress important words.

Comprehension

Write your answer to each question on the lines below.

1. At the beginning of the play, why is Miss Fishpenny sad?

_____

_____

2. Which do you prefer—a tall tale or a science fiction story? Why?

_____

_____

3. When Leo says it has snowed at least three feet, why does Miss Fishpenny think he is exaggerating? _____

_____

4. How did Paul Bunyan and Babe save lives?

_____

_____

5. Were you surprised by how the play ended? Why?

_____

_____

6. What did you learn about tall tales in the play?

_____

_____

7. Which character in the play is most like you? Why?

_____

_____

The Tallest Tale Ever
Readers' Theater 3, SV 9781419031687

Vocabulary

Write each vocabulary word on the line where it belongs.

entertain   brilliant   unbelievable   exaggerate   humorous

1. When you say that something is a lot bigger than it really is, you

   _____.

2. Stories about space monsters and little green people are

   _____.

3. People laugh at jokes because jokes are _____.

4. On a sunny day, the sky is usually _____ blue.

5. Grandma will _____ us with her stories.

Extension

1. With a partner, talk about what you would do if you met Paul Bunyan.

   • Would you ask him to prove how strong he is?

   • Would you ask him to do something for you?

   • Would you ask him to tell you about his adventures?

2. Write and read aloud an original tall tale.

   • Make sure your tall tale hero is "larger-than-life."

   • Use words like *biggest*, *strongest*, *fastest*, and *smartest*.

   • Have your hero do something that would be impossible for a real person to do.

   Use the Story Map on page 12.

Don't Be Afraid

Summary

"Don't Be Afraid" is a four-character play about Keisha, who is getting ready to talk to her class about her epilepsy.

Meet the Players

Character	Reading Level
Mrs. Johnson	2.5
Marcus	2.3
Keisha	3.3
Christina	0.9

Fluency Focus
Reading with Word Accuracy

Comprehension Focus
Building Background

Vocabulary
dangerous
embarrass
epilepsy
medicine
seizure

Set the Stage

Teacher Read Aloud *page 101*

This selection is about therapy dogs, which assist people with disabilities. Read the selection aloud. Encourage students to follow along, noting your blending of word parts.

Get Ready

Vocabulary *page 102*

Use this page to introduce vocabulary. Discuss the Vocabulary Think Tank question and have students make a list of when medicines can be helpful and when they can be dangerous.

Fluency and Comprehension Warm-Ups *pages 102–103*

Review these pages with students. Use the following for students who need additional help with the concepts:

- **Reading with Word Accuracy** When you come to a large, unfamiliar word, break it into smaller word parts. Then blend the parts together to say the word. Look at this word from paragraph 4 of the Read Aloud: *rehabilitation*. Repeat the word parts together: *re—ha—bil—i—ta—tion*. Now blend the parts to read the word: rehabilitation.

- **Building Background** The first part of building background is thinking about the topic and what you already know about it. For example, you may already know that one kind of dog that helps people is a guide dog. Then think about what else you should learn to better understand the topic.

Read Aloud Tip

After reading the selection, practice the fluency focus of **reading with word accuracy**. Write the following words from paragraph 2 of the Read Aloud on the board: *organizations, therapy, disabilities*. For each word, model blending and putting word parts together. Then point to words randomly and have volunteers read them aloud.

Don't Be Afraid *pages 104–110*

Independent Practice

Set up the groups and assign each student a part. Then have students read through their assigned parts once before small group practice begins.

Small Group Practice

Assemble the groups. You may want to use the following rehearsal schedule. Each rehearsal, which should involve a complete oral read-through, has an activity to guide students.

1. First Rehearsal: Guide students through a play preview by reading the title, character list, and stage directions and by viewing the pictures. Invite volunteers to make predictions about the play based on the title "Don't Be Afraid." Students will then read together as a group for the first time.

2. Vocabulary Rehearsal: Encourage students to locate the vocabulary words in the play. Then challenge each student to compose a sentence that includes two vocabulary words, such as "Taking too much *medicine* can be *dangerous*." Have students share their sentences with a partner.

3. Fluency Rehearsal: Reading with Word Accuracy Before this rehearsal, review the fluency instruction on page 102, explaining that word accuracy means reading the words correctly. After the rehearsal, ask each student to choose one Fluency Tip and apply it to an example from the play. For example, the tip on page 106 could be used with the words *epilepsy* or *interested*, which appear on page 105.

4. Comprehension Rehearsal: Building Background After this rehearsal, have students work in groups to create T-Charts to record what they know and what they want to find out.

5. Final Rehearsal: Observe this rehearsal, focusing on students' ability to read with word accuracy. For example, do students recognize and pronounce both small words in compound words like *playground* and *everyone*? When needed, model blending word parts for students having difficulty.

Performance

This is your opportunity to sit back, relax, and enjoy the performance. Encourage students to have fun while performing!

Curtain Call *pages 111–112*

Assign these questions and activities for students to complete in a group or independently.

Vocabulary Tip

For more vocabulary practice, have students discuss the following:

- Which is more **dangerous**—a kitten or a lion? Why?

- How do you act when you are **embarrassed**?

- When might someone need **medicine**?

Don't Be Afraid

Set the Stage
Teacher Read Aloud

Imagine not being able to do some of the things you do naturally every day. Imagine that you are not able to open a door, turn on a light, or hear the phone ring. You would need help to do these things.

Some organizations provide **therapy** dogs to help people with disabilities. The dogs are called therapy dogs because the word *therapy* comes from a word that means "assistance." The dogs are specially trained to perform tasks that people with disabilities have difficulty performing themselves.

The dogs are trained to pull a wheelchair, respond when someone has a seizure, open doors, flip switches to turn on lights, and more. Hearing dogs are trained to respond to such sounds as a ringing telephone, a crying baby, and a knock at the door.

Some dogs are used in schools, rehabilitation programs, and hospitals. These dogs also help bring joy and companionship to people going through challenging times.

In this play you will read about a girl with epilepsy. Use the vocabulary and warm-ups to help you get ready.

Vocabulary

Read and review these vocabulary words to prepare you for reading this play. Which words are nouns? Write the letter *n* next to the nouns.

dangerous—likely to cause harm

embarrass—to cause to feel nervous or uneasy

epilepsy (EH puh lep see)—a disorder in which a person has seizures

medicine—something used to treat a disease or relieve pain

seizure (SEE zher)—a sudden attack, often causing the body to shake

> **VOCABULARY THINK TANK**
>
> Can medicine be dangerous?

Fluency Warm-Up

Reading with Word Accuracy

Fluent readers take the time to read with **accuracy**. They put sounds and word parts together to read more smoothly. You can improve the way you read by blending sounds and word parts together.

Remember to look for smaller word parts. Blend the sounds together to make a word.

> **FLUENCY PRACTICE**
>
> Try to read these larger words. Break them into smaller word parts. Then read them as a whole word.
>
> 1. discontinue   dis-con-tin-ue
> 2. intelligent   in-tell-i-gent
> 3. accuracy   ac-cur-a-cy
> 4. represent   rep-re-sent

Comprehension Warm-Up

Building Background

Building background will help you better understand the story. To build background knowledge, you must think about what you know about the topic. Then you need to ask what you need to know to understand the topic better.

A dictionary, a book on the topic, or asking someone are ways to help you build background.

COMPREHENSION TIP

As you read, ask yourself questions like these below.

1. How much do I know about this topic?

2. What information do I need to help me understand this?

3. Where can I look to find this information?

Readers' Theater 3, SV 9781419031687

Readers' Theater

Presents
Don't Be Afraid
by
Justine Dunn

Cast
(in order of appearance)

Mrs. Johnson _____

Marcus _____

Keisha _____

Christina _____

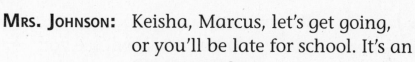

MRS. JOHNSON: Keisha, Marcus, let's get going, or you'll be late for school. It's an important day.

MARCUS: We'll be right down, Mom. Keisha is still getting dressed.

KEISHA: I am not! I'm ready. I'm coming. I was just getting my doll to bring to school.

MARCUS: Aren't you a little old to be bringing a doll to school?

KEISHA: I'm not bringing it to play with, silly. I'm bringing it because I'm going to use it when I talk to my class about **epilepsy**.

MRS. JOHNSON: I'm so proud of you for sharing your story with your friends at school, Keisha. They will be interested in learning more about it.

MARCUS: I was only teasing you, Keisha. I'm proud of you, too.

KEISHA: I know, Marcus. You like to tease me a lot, but you also help me when I have **seizures**. You're a great big brother.

MRS. JOHNSON: OK, you two. Let's get going. Keisha, Marcus and I will see you in your class a little later to help with your speech.

CHRISTINA: *(waving)* Hi, Keisha! Come sit by me!

KEISHA: Hi, Christina. I'm so nervous about talking in front of the class today.

CHRISTINA: Remember what you told me when I was scared about you being sick? You said, "Don't be afraid."

KEISHA: You're right. Besides, my mom and my brother will be here to help me.

MRS. JOHNSON: *(enters the classroom)* Hello, Christina. It's nice to see you. How are you?

CHRISTINA: Hi, Mrs. Johnson. I'm fine. Look, here comes Marcus.

MARCUS: *(enters the classroom)* Hey, Chris-tiny.

MRS. JOHNSON: *(angrily)* Marcus! Don't be rude. I expect you to behave.

CHRISTINA: It's OK, Mrs. Johnson. I know Marcus is only kidding. He really likes me.

> **FLUENCY TIP**
>
> When you see large words, try to break them down into smaller word parts. For example, *im-port-ant*.

Don't Be Afraid
Readers' Theater 3, SV 9781419031687

KEISHA: Marcus, please don't **embarrass** me. I need your help today during my speech.

MARCUS: Oh, all right. What do you need me to do?

MRS. JOHNSON: You should explain how you help Keisha when she has a seizure.

CHRISTINA: Yes, Marcus. I learned a lot from watching you. Now I'm not scared anymore.

MARCUS: I used to get mad that Keisha got a lot of attention. Then I realized that she wasn't doing any of this on purpose.

KEISHA: Not at all. If I had a wish, it would be that I didn't have epilepsy.

CHRISTINA: I'm just glad you told me how to help.

MRS. JOHNSON: Most children would be afraid if they saw someone have a seizure.

KEISHA: I remember the first time I had a seizure at school. My friends were really scared.

MARCUS: We were outside on the playground, and I saw Keisha fall to the ground and start shaking.

Don't Be Afraid
Readers' Theater 3, SV 9781419031687

CHRISTINA: I didn't know what to do.

MRS. JOHNSON: I'm so glad you were both there with Keisha, since I couldn't be.

KEISHA: I don't remember much after that, except for waking up and seeing everyone.

MARCUS: I ran over to you and told everyone to stay calm. That's one of the most important things to do.

MRS. JOHNSON: Yes, it is, Marcus. However, it is not always easy.

MARCUS: I asked the teacher to look at her watch. If a seizure lasts more than five minutes, you should call for help.

KEISHA: Most of my seizures only last for a few minutes, but it's important to keep track.

CHRISTINA: It felt like a lot longer than that!

MRS. JOHNSON: I know what you mean, Christina.

> **FLUENCY TIP**
>
> Some words have an *-ing* ending. When you break a word into smaller parts to make it easier to read, the *-ing* ending is one of those word parts. For example, *watch-ing, do-ing, act-ing.*

Don't Be Afraid
Readers' Theater 3, SV 9781419031687

MARCUS: When a person is having a seizure, you should not try to stop him or her from shaking. It can be **dangerous** for both you and the person.

CHRISTINA: I asked the other kids to step back and give Keisha some room.

KEISHA: It's natural for people to want to see what's going on, but I don't exactly want everyone staring at me during a seizure.

MRS. JOHNSON: I wish your seizures only happened at home. Then I would be there.

KEISHA: The trouble is, you never know when a seizure is going to happen.

MARCUS: I had heard that people who are having a seizure can swallow their tongue. Dr. Wong told us that that is not true.

KEISHA: The **medicines** I take help control my seizures. I eat certain types of foods that can help me, too.

MRS. JOHNSON: I'm happy that those things are working. Some people have to have an operation.

MARCUS: Some people worry that they will catch epilepsy. That's not true, either.

CHRISTINA: Most people who have it are born with it.

KEISHA: I am hoping that by telling the people in my class about epilepsy, they will understand more of what I go through.

CHRISTINA: Maybe fewer kids will be afraid, too.

MRS. JOHNSON: You're very brave, Keisha, and I'm so proud of you. You're my hero.

CHRISTINA: I'm so glad we're friends!

KEISHA: Thanks to all of you for your help. It really means a lot to me that I can count on you.

MARCUS: Yeah, you're not bad for a little sister, even if you still play with dolls.

KEISHA: Watch out, Marcus, or I'll tell my whole class that you said you were proud of me this morning!

(The group laughs.)

> **FLUENCY TIP**
>
> Notice the common letters in the words *count* and *proud*? The [ou] sound in both words is the same.

Comprehension

Write your answer to each question on the lines below.

1. Why is Keisha nervous?

_____

_____

2. What are two things you should do if someone has a seizure?

_____

_____

3. Why does Keisha want to talk to her class about epilepsy?

_____

_____

4. Do you think Christina is a good friend? Why or why not?

_____

_____

5. What were two things you learned about epilepsy from this play?

_____

_____

6. Do you think Keisha sometimes feels embarrassed about her seizures?

_____

_____

7. Do you think Keisha's friends will still be afraid if she has a seizure? Why or why not?

_____

_____

Vocabulary

Finish the paragraph by writing a vocabulary word on each line.

| embarrass | medicine | epilepsy | seizure | dangerous |

Some people have a disease called (1) _____. A person with this disease can have a (2) _____. When that happens, the person often shakes. This might (3) _____ the person, but it is not really (4) _____. People with epilepsy take (5) _____ to control the disease.

Extension

1. In a small group, discuss what you would do if someone at school had a seizure.

   • Would you stay calm?

   • Would you call for help?

   • Would you be afraid?

2. With a partner, do some research about a famous person who had a disability and write a story about him or her. Then read your story aloud to the class. Choose a person below.

   • Helen Keller

   • Christopher Reeve

   • Franklin Delano Roosevelt

   Use the web on page 13 to help you.

Dolley Madison Saves George!

Summary

"Dolley Madison Saves George!" is a six-character play about Dolley Madison's efforts to save important papers and paintings when British troops invaded Washington.

Meet the Players

Character	Reading Level
Narrator	5.7
President Madison	2.4
Dolley Madison	2.7
French John	1.3
British Soldier 1	0.9
British Soldier 2	1.2

Fluency Focus
Using Expression

Comprehension Focus
Asking Questions

Vocabulary
burning
cannon
replace
shame
soldiers
trunk

Set the Stage

Teacher Read Aloud   *page 115*
This Read Aloud is about the White House. As you read the selection to the students, make your voice sound excited when reading about the design contest and sad when reading about the fire.

Get Ready

Read Aloud Tip

Read the selection once. Then reread paragraph 3 of the Read Aloud, using exaggerated expression to indicate feelings of sorrow over the burning of the White House. Introduce the fluency focus, **using expression**, by asking students to identify the emotion they think you were trying to express.

Vocabulary   *page 116*
Use this page to introduce vocabulary. Discuss the Vocabulary Think Tank question, focusing on having students list three ways household items lost in a fire might be replaced.

Fluency and Comprehension Warm-Ups   *pages 116–117*
Review these pages with students. Use the following for students who need additional help with the concepts:

- **Using Expression** As you read, change your voice to give clues about a character's feelings. Read the sentence on the board to yourself: *I am so worried that I'll strike out in today's game.* Think about how this person is feeling. Now read the sentence aloud.

- **Asking Questions** Before reading, good readers ask themselves what they already know about a topic. During reading, they ask what might happen next. After reading, they ask, "What did I learn?" As you look at the Read Aloud, put a sticky note next to a sentence that answers, "What did I learn?"

Dolley Madison Saves George! *pages 118–124*

Independent Practice

Set up the groups and assign each student a part. Then have students read through their assigned parts once before small group practice begins.

Small Group Practice

Assemble the groups. You may want to use the following rehearsal schedule. Each rehearsal, which should involve a complete oral read-through, has an activity to guide students.

1. First Rehearsal: Guide students to preview the play by reading the title, character list, and stage directions. Invite a volunteer to use the title to predict George's identity. Invite students to then read together as a group for the first time.

2. Vocabulary Rehearsal: Direct students to locate and list on index cards the vocabulary words used in the play. Have them turn the cards facedown and take turns choosing a card and pantomiming the word for other members of the group to guess.

3. Fluency Rehearsal: Using Expression Before the rehearsal begins, invite students to review the Fluency Tips by alternating reading them aloud. Then encourage students to have fun by overacting—exaggerating characters' feelings. Explain that the narrator can overact by using a deep voice and reading the lines as if giving an important news broadcast.

4. Comprehension Rehearsal: Asking Questions After this rehearsal, have students work together to answer this question: What are we supposed to learn from this play? Ask them to list at least three facts they think the author wanted to teach through the play.

5. Final Rehearsal: Observe this rehearsal, focusing on students' expression. For example, when reading French John's line on page 120, "I could put a cannon at the gate!" does the student read with excitement?

Performance

This is your opportunity to sit back, relax, and enjoy the performance. Encourage students to have fun while performing!

Curtain Call *pages 125–126*

Assign these questions and activities for students to complete in a group or independently.

Vocabulary Tip

For more vocabulary practice, have students discuss the following:

- Which would make you feel **shame**: lying to a friend or helping a family member?

- Would an elephant fit into a **trunk**? Would a book?

- What do you own that would be hard to **replace**?

---

www.harcourtschoolsupply.com

114

Dolley Madison Saves George!
Readers' Theater 3, SV 9781419031687

Dolley Madison Saves George!

Set the Stage
Teacher Read Aloud

The White House, located in Washington, D.C., is the official home and office of the President of the United States. All of the United States presidents except George Washington have lived in the White House.

The history of the White House started in 1792. A contest was held to see who could come up with the best design. James Hoban won the design contest and a $500 prize. President George Washington helped choose the building site. The actual building began in 1792. John Adams, the second president, was the first to move into the White House in 1800.

The White House was burned during the War of 1812, during the presidency of James Madison. Hoban worked on the reconstruction of the White House. By 1817, the White House was ready for then President James Monroe.

There are 132 rooms and 35 bathrooms in the White House. It also has a swimming pool, a movie theater, a bowling alley, a basketball court, and a jogging track.

The White House is a symbol of the United States, its government, and its people. This historic site in Washington, D.C., attracts more than 1.5 million visitors every year.

In this play, you will read about what happened in Washington, D.C., in 1814. Use the vocabulary and warm-ups to help you get ready.

Vocabulary

Read and review these words with a partner. This will help prepare you for reading this play.

burning—destroying with fire

cannon—a large gun that shoots cannonballs

replace—to take the place of something lost

shame—a painful, embarrassing feeling

soldiers—people who fight in an army

trunk—a large case for holding clothes and other things

> **VOCABULARY THINK TANK**
>
> If a home had burned, how would the people replace the things lost in the fire?

Fluency Warm-Up

Using Expression

Fluent readers read with **expression**. Expression means to have feeling in your voice. Try to show how your character is feeling — happy or sad or mad!

What clues are in the text that help you understand feelings? Maybe you see an exclamation point or all capital letters. Or maybe you just have to use your imagination. Then change your voice to express loud or soft feelings.

FLUENCY PRACTICE

Read these sentences three times. Sound happy the first time, sad the second time, and mad the third time.

1. She gave me a slice of bread.

2. Look at that.

3. That is mine.

Dolley Madison Saves George!
Readers' Theater 3, SV 9781419031687

Comprehension Warm-Up

Asking Questions

It is a good idea to **ask questions** before, during, and after you read. Asking questions will help you think more about the story and understand it better.

Make sure you don't just read words. You need to be thinking about what you are reading. Think about what is happening and what might happen next. Ask yourself what the author is trying to teach you or tell you.

COMPREHENSION TIP

As you read, ask yourself questions like these. Think about the answers.

- What does this sentence mean?
- Why is this character acting this way?
- What am I supposed to learn from this?

www.harcourtschoolsupply.com

117

Dolley Madison Saves George!
Readers' Theater 3, SV 9781419031687

Readers' Theater

Presents
Dolley Madison Saves George!

by
Carol M. Elliott

Cast
(in order of appearance)

Narrator   _____

President Madison   _____

Dolley Madison   _____

French John   _____

British Soldier 1   _____

British Soldier 2   _____

www.harcourtschoolsupply.com

118

Dolley Madison Saves George!
Readers' Theater 3, SV 9781419031687

NARRATOR: It is Monday morning, August 22nd, 1814. The British Army is advancing toward Washington, D.C. The United States Army is preparing for battle. President James Madison and First Lady Dolley Madison are deciding what to do.

PRES. MADISON: I need to join the general. I have to help plan this battle. But I worry about leaving you here alone.

DOLLEY MADISON: Do not worry about me. I will be fine. Besides, I am not alone. The servants are here.

PRES. MADISON: Are you sure you want to stay? Many people are leaving the city. You could go, too.

DOLLEY MADISON: I want to stay here at the White House. It is our home. I am not afraid. I believe that you and the army will beat the British. And when you return, we will have a wonderful dinner for you and the officers.

PRES. MADISON: I will try to return in two to three days. Please take care of yourself, my dear.

NARRATOR: The next day President Madison sent a message to his wife.

FRENCH JOHN: This message just came. It is from the president.

DOLLEY MADISON: *(reading)* It says the enemy seems stronger than had been reported. He wants us to be ready to leave. He is afraid if the British do get through, they will destroy the city.

❋ **FRENCH JOHN:** What do you want us to do? Should we prepare to leave? Or should we prepare to fight? I could put a **cannon** at the gate!

DOLLEY MADISON: I suppose we must get ready to leave, but I am not leaving yet. I still believe our army will win and we will have a party tomorrow night.

❋ **FLUENCY TIP**

How is French John feeling? Change your voice to show his feelings as he asks Dolley Madison what to do.

FRENCH JOHN: I hope you're right. But I heard that the **soldiers** who were supposed to guard the city have left.

NARRATOR: Dolley and the servants packed several **trunks**. Then Dolley sat down to write a letter to her sister.

DOLLEY MADISON: *(writing)* I have packed the president's important papers in trunks. Our things must be left behind as there aren't enough wagons to move everything. Our friends are all gone. I am not leaving, though. I want to wait for Mr. Madison.

NARRATOR: The next day was Wednesday, August 24th. Dolley Madison had the table set for forty people. She had the servants prepare a dinner. She still hoped that the U.S. Army would win. Then she continued her letter to her sister.

Dolley Madison Saves George!
Readers' Theater 3, SV 9781419031687

DOLLEY MADISON: *(writing)* Since sunrise, I have used my spyglass to look for my dear husband and his friends. But they do not come. There has been a battle in a town a few miles from here. I can hear the sound of the cannon!

FRENCH JOHN: Two messengers are here covered with dust. They say we are to leave—now! The enemy is almost here!

✻ **DOLLEY MADISON:** I will not leave without the large painting of General Washington. He is the father of our country, and the picture must be saved.

FRENCH JOHN: But that picture is fixed to the wall. We can't take the time to undo that.

✻ **DOLLEY MADISON:** Then break the frame! I will not leave without the painting!

NARRATOR: Finally, Dolley Madison and the servants left the White House. They had saved the picture of George Washington. The British soldiers arrived a few hours later. The table was still set.

> ✻ **FLUENCY TIP**
>
> How is Dolley Madison feeling? Use loudness in your voice to express her strong feelings.

www.harcourtschoolsupply.com

122

Dolley Madison Saves George!
Readers' Theater 3, SV 9781419031687

British soldier 1: So this is their president's palace.

British soldier 2: And look here. They must have been planning a party.

British soldier 1: It would be a **shame** to waste all this food. Let's eat!

Narrator: After the soldiers had eaten, they took a look around the White House.

British soldier 1: This White House isn't so special. Look at this broken frame hanging here on the wall.

British soldier 2: Yes, we will be doing them a favor by **burning** this place down!

Narrator: The enemy soldiers laughed as they set fire to the White House. Then they set fire to many other buildings. Soon the city was burning. Three days later, the Madisons returned to their home.

Dolley Madison Saves George!
Readers' Theater 3, SV 9781419031687

DOLLEY MADISON: What a shame! Our lovely home is gone!

PRES. MADISON: Oh, Dolley, I am sorry that the army could not stop them.

DOLLEY MADISON: The most important thing, my dear husband, is that you are safe. We will rebuild the White House. The British will not win.

PRES. MADISON: I suppose we can **replace** most of what was lost. Thank you for saving my important papers. Ah, but the picture of George Washington! How will we ever replace that?

DOLLEY MADISON: We will only need to replace the frame. We had to break it to remove the painting, but the picture was saved!

PRES. MADISON: That's great! What a wonderful and brave woman you are!

FLUENCY TIP

President Madison's feelings change on this page. Express this change from sad to proud in your reading.

Comprehension

Write your answer to each question on the lines below.

1. Why was President Madison worried about leaving his wife?

   _____

   _____

2. How did French John help Dolley Madison?

   _____

   _____

3. What did the British soldiers do when they saw the table set for dinner?

   _____

   _____

4. Why did Dolley Madison tell French John to break the frame on

   Washington's picture? _____

   _____

5. Why did Dolley Madison feel she needed to save the painting of George

   Washington?_____

   _____

6. What would you ask the author if you could talk to her?

   _____

   _____

7. Why do you think the British wanted to burn the White House?

   _____

   _____

Vocabulary

Write the vocabulary word that answers the question.

| trunk | soldiers | cannon | shame | burning | replace |

1. Which word describes people who fight for their country? _____

2. Which word names a weapon? _____

3. Which word can be a suitcase or part of a tree? _____

4. Which word is the opposite of *pride*? _____

5. Which word can describe a fire? _____

Extension

1. What would you have done if you were Dolley Madison and the British were coming? With a partner, talk about what you would have done.

   • How long would you have stayed in the White House?

   • What would you have tried to save?

   Write a short play telling your ideas.

2. With a partner, do some research on Washington, D.C., and write a story about it. Then read your story aloud to the class. Choose a topic below.

   • Write a story about one of the famous people or buildings in the city.

   • Write a story about what it would be like, or is like, to live in D.C.

   Use the web on page 13 to help you.

3. Research the major wars in United States history. Place them on the time line on page 14.

Answer Key

The No-Sleep Sleepover

Comprehension, page 27

(Suggested responses for 3, 4, and 6)

1. Bruno and his father sleep at night and are awake during the day.
2. Raymond and Orville usually hunt for food at night.
3. Father might fix berries for Bruno, nuts for Sergio and Raymond, and a mouse for Orville.
4. Some animals sleep during the day and hunt at night. Owls eat mice and small birds.
5. Responses will vary.
6. Bruno Bear and his father find out that Bruno's friends have very different eating and sleeping habits.

Vocabulary, page 28

1. adventure
2. bury
3. guest
4. twitching
5. favorite

Plant and Gator Soup

Comprehension, page 41

(Suggested responses for 2, 3, 5, and 6)

1. Responses will vary.
2. The Everglades is a national park in south Florida. It is home to animals such as alligators and snakes. It is also home to plants such as bladderworts, sawgrass, and the coontie.
3. The play is about a family that goes for a boat trip through the Everglades.
4. A bladderwort gets food by trapping small animals in tiny hollow bags.
5. Max and Sarah saw bugs, alligators, and carnivorous plants.

6. The bladderwort is adapted to living in the water because it can trap water fleas that live there.

Vocabulary, page 42

1. clever
2. adapt
3. wetland
4. Everglades
5. carnivorous

A Day at the Weather Center

Comprehension, page 55

(Suggested responses)

1. Forecasters use radar to track thunderstorms, hurricanes, and other bad weather.
2. There are many weather centers because each one tracks the weather for one part of the country.
3. Mr. Wilder has to end the tour because a weather system is moving through, and he has to send information to other weather centers.
4. Falling air pressure means bad weather is coming. There are hundreds of weather centers across the United States.
5. Maya wasn't so scared of tornadoes anymore because she knows that the weather centers keep track of weather systems and send the information to TV and radio stations to keep the public informed.
6. Zack was bored at the beginning of the play, but he was excited at the end.
7. Taking a field trip like this one is a good idea because it helps students understand science much better.

Vocabulary, page 56

1. operator
2. radar

3. atmosphere
4. data
5. forecast

The Fourth Rock from the Sun

Comprehension, page 69

(Suggested responses for 3, 4, and 6)

1. Mars and Earth are closest together once every two years.
2. Responses will vary.
3. Mars has water, it is colder than Earth, and it has different gases in its atmosphere.
4. They grow plants to eat.
5. Responses will vary.
6. There are 687 days in a year on Mars. There is a volcano on Mars that is three times taller than the tallest mountain on Earth. Mars may have had water in the past.
7. Responses will vary.

Vocabulary, page 70

Answers from top to bottom should read as follows: 4, 5, 1, 3, 6, 2

The Worst Thanksgiving Ever

Comprehension, page 83

(Suggested responses for 1, 4, and 6)

1. Thanksgiving is different because Dad isn't there, there is no electricity, and the family is cooking food in the fireplace.
2. It means that the smell is making everyone hungry.
3. Eddy would rather get wood than peel potatoes.
4. Without electricity, the family can't use the stove to cook dinner, and there are no lights.
5. Responses will vary.

Answer Key
Readers' Theater 3, SV 9781419031687

6. This was "the best Thanksgiving ever" because it made the family realize the true meaning of Thanksgiving.

7. Responses will vary.

Vocabulary, page 84

Answers from top to bottom should read as follows: 4, 5, 6, 3, 2, 1

The Tallest Tale Ever

Comprehension, page 97

(Suggested responses for 3 and 6)

1. Miss Fishpenny is sad because the bad weather means the Storytelling Festival has to be cancelled.

2. Responses will vary.

3. Miss Fishpenny thinks Leo is exaggerating because he often does exaggerate.

4. Paul Bunyan and Babe clear the snow off the roof before it collapses.

5. Responses will vary.

6. Tall tales are humorous. They are exaggerated history. They are based on things that actually happened and are about people who actually lived.

7. Responses will vary.

Vocabulary, page 98

1. exaggerate
2. unbelievable
3. humorous
4. brilliant
5. entertain

Don't Be Afraid

Comprehension, page 111

(Suggested responses)

1. Keisha is nervous because she is going to talk in front of the whole class.

2. If someone has a seizure, you should stay calm and give the person some room.

3. Keisha wants her classmates to know what to expect if she has a seizure.

4. Christina is a good friend because she wants to know how to help Keisha.

5. Epilepsy causes seizures. People cannot catch epilepsy from people who have it.

6. Keisha sometimes feels embarrassed about her seizures because everyone stares at her.

7. Keisha's friends may still be afraid when she has a seizure, but they will understand what it is and what they should do.

Vocabulary, page 112

1. epilepsy
2. seizure
3. embarrass
4. dangerous
5. medicine

Dolley Madison Saves George!

Comprehension, page 125

(Suggested responses for 1, 2, 5, and 7)

1. President Madison was worried because many people had left the city and his wife would be alone.

2. French John got the painting out of the frame for Dolley Madison.

3. The soldiers sat down and ate the food on the table.

4. Dolley Madison told French John to break the frame because that was the only way to get the picture off the wall.

5. Dolley Madison felt that she needed to save the painting of George Washington because he is the father of the United States.

6. Responses will vary.

7. The British wanted to burn the White House to destroy everything that was there and to make it harder for the United States to win the war.

Vocabulary, page 126

1. soldiers
2. cannon
3. trunk
4. shame
5. burning